THE SECRET LIFE OF ORGANIZATIONS

Dr Shalini Lal is an organizational development thinker, problem solver and consultant. She is the founder of Infinity OD, a consulting firm that works with client organizations to help build their leadership, culture and capabilities. She was named as an 'Exceptional leader of excellence' by the Women Economic Forum for 2018. She is a graduate of St. Stephen's College, Delhi, has an MBA from IIM-A and a PhD from UCLA. In a career spanning over 25 years she has worked in senior HR roles, such as director HR with Deutsche Bank, chief HR officer at Escorts Agri-machinery and chief (organizational development) at Airtel. She is also an independent board director and a sought out columnist and guest speaker. She lives in New Delhi with her husband, two children, three dogs and one cat.

Dr Pradnya Parasher is the founder and CEO of ThreeFish Consulting, with more than 20 years of experience in strategic HR, talent management, executive assessment and coaching. Pradnya has a PhD in industrial/organizational psychology from the University of South Florida. She helps leaders and leadership teams understand their psychological DNA and adapt their behaviours to become even more effective. She has coached early-career professionals and senior leaders to successfully navigate critical career transitions. Pradnya has lived in the United States and India, and worked with leaders across Asia, Europe and the US. She believes that one can live authentically and still achieve career success.

'I wish I had read this book thirty-five years ago when I began my career. When you begin your career, you never realise that there is so much more to doing well in organizations. In fact, there is a science and art to understanding organizations and how to navigate them. This book covers so many really important topics, ones that even most business schools miss while teaching. I highly recommend this to young professionals starting out on their careers.' – Sanjeev Bikhchandani, Co-founder, Naukri.com

'[This] book is like a wise old friend, guide and mentor. Highly recommended [for] every young person starting their career!' – Rashmi Bansal, bestselling author of *Stay Hungry Stay Foolish*

'This book truly unravels the "secrets" of success in today's organizations. Very insightful and extremely practical, the authors have done a fabulous job in diagnosing organizations, and bringing to the fore the talent management practices in vogue. More importantly, they have put together a wonderful set of tips for aspiring people to navigate these successfully. An excellent guide for success in our times – a must-read for everyone keen to get an insight into the working of our organizations!' – Krish Shankar, Executive Vice President and Group Head of HR Development, Infosys

'Lal and Parasher bring a structured approach to [having a] great work life. At a time when work is radically changing... *The Secret Life of Organizations* is a great read not only for professionals starting their career but also for professionals looking to accelerate it.' – Ester Martinez, CEO, People Matters

'[The book] reads like an engrossing novel, peeling layer by layer of the mysteries of life within an organization. The book is a gold mine of simple tips, not just for job aspirants, but for people higher up on the corporate ladder...and for those that belong to the unorganized sector. [The authors] give valuable insights into the world of organizations through personal experiences and relatable real-life examples... In fact, it [is a] recipe for success in life itself.' – Renuka Shahane, actor, director, scriptwriter

THE SECRET LIFE OF ORGANIZATIONS

Invisible rules of success for
the young Indian professional

SHALINI LAL
PRADNYA PARASHER

hachette
INDIA

First published in 2019 by Hachette India
(Registered name: Hachette Book Publishing India Pvt. Ltd)
An Hachette UK company
www.hachetteindia.com

SRD

Book illustrations by Mistunee Chowdhury

ISBN 978-93-88322-11-9

Hachette Book Publishing India Pvt. Ltd
4th & 5th Floors, Corporate Centre,
Plot No. 94, Sector 44, Gurugram – 122003, India

Typeset in Adobe Garamond 11.5/15
by InoSoft Systems, Noida

Printed and bound in India
by Manipal Technologies Limited, Manipal

MIX
Paper from responsible sources
FSC www.fsc.org FSC™ C104740

To my dear children, Aashna and Arjun. You are the reason I wrote this book. I can see how talented you are, and as you join the workforce I want you to be smarter than your mom ever was. More than anything else, I want for you the joy of moments when time stands still as you and your work become one.

Shalini

This book is for my children, Ved and Shruti. And for the millions of youngsters who graduate every year from schools and colleges across India, I hope you find joy and fulfilment in building the careers that you choose to build.

Pradnya

CONTENTS

FOUR: LOOK BEYOND

INTRODUCTION

Knowledge is power.

What would you say if you were told that doing well in the organizational world is as much about understanding your organization as it is about understanding your job? Or that, unless you have a mentor to show you the ropes fairly early on in your career, it's going to take a lot of piecing together of information to figure out how to go about climbing the ladder of success.

That's a little daunting, right?

While some of you may be incredibly talented and find your footing in an organization effortlessly even without a mentor, this book is for people who are clueless the way we, the authors, were when we first started working. We had both been good students and excelled in school and college where the rules of success were reasonably clear. But when we entered the organizational world, we soon realized that there was a big difference between studying organizations and negotiating your way through them. In fact, unlike school or college, there was no clear set of rules to follow. Gone were the straightforward weekly tests or annual exams that you could simply ace. These were replaced by very ambiguous criteria. Of course, we had job descriptions and annual goals to guide us. Yet, most of the time, we had the gnawing feeling that these goals or criteria were only part of what mattered. We could see that there was far more to being successful than what was being openly discussed in our workplaces. But as newbies, we didn't know what that 'something more' was or how to understand it.

This is why we wrote this book. This book is for anyone who is just starting out in their career and wants to understand the invisible rules by which organizations operate. What we want to share with you is what we wish we had known when we started out in our first jobs – things like how to understand your organization first through its culture and business, how to build work relationships and how to design a career that brings you success and joy.

What's the big secret?

Ever noticed how great gamers manage to keep moving up levels of a game by working out the secret passages and the secret rules?

In some ways, building an organizational career is similar. There are secret passages and invisible rules for success, which, for the most part, you have to figure out on your own. When you are beginning your career, these rules seem to be hidden from plain sight. Even those who are using these rules may not understand them very well. What's more, unlike a video game, you do not get an unlimited number of attempts to figure things out. For starters, there are often consequences for your actions, and for another, you don't always get immediate feedback.

As a young professional, for instance, you won't immediately be part of discussions regarding promotions or any talent councils. Consequently, you will not necessarily know how you and your performance are being discussed at these important meetings. Yet, you will be affected by what these conversations say about you. Here, we share with you what we have learnt from our ringside view of these discussions.

How universal are these secrets?

In our experience – *quite universal.*

Whether it is India or Korea or the US you are trying to build your career in, you will need to understand your organization and navigate it. For this, you will need to understand your organization's culture and its business, and figure out how to build relationships and use influence – wherever you are.

The maxims we discuss will apply irrespective of whether you are in the technology industry, the finance industry, the pharmaceutical industry or even in a not-for-profit. The questions you will need to ask to decode and navigate your way through the organization will remain pretty much the same. What will vary considerably are the answers you will find.

We ourselves have worked (and are working) with organizations in many parts of the world, across many different industries. This universality of key questions allows us (now as consultants) to quickly understand our clients who are from very varied environments, and design interventions that will work for them. Each of you will, in all likelihood, be building your career across a few different organizations too. And we hope this book gives you a useful framework to help you in navigating your organizations effectively.

It has taken us several decades of understanding organizations as practitioners and academics to be able to articulate these guidelines. Both of us have PhDs in either organizational science (Shalini) or organizational psychology (Pradnya). We have also worked in many different roles in Indian and global organizations. It is this shared background that brought us together to write this book.

Consider this book your cheat sheet to organizational life.

What are we going to talk about?

We will start by helping you understand how to understand your organization better. How can you read and understand the culture of your organization and its implications? What can your organization's stories tell you about what it values? Why should you care about what your organization values? How can you properly understand the business of the organization? These are a few of the topics that we will explore.

We will also look at ways that will help you navigate your organizational world better. We will discuss the tricky business of managing your organizational relationships – with your boss and with your peers, as well as how to understand and deal with power and politics and gender differences. We think each of these chapters has lessons that can have a huge impact on how successfully your career plays out. Speaking as idealists, we also hope that this understanding will in turn help you build better organizations.

We will then proceed to tell you about how you can manage yourself. How can you better understand yourself so that you make choices that work for you? How can you learn to shift gears each time you are faced with a career transition – a new role, a new organization or even a new country?

Finally, we will attempt to help you look beyond your immediate reality and present. We are living in a world that is very quickly morphing into something new that we don't yet fully understand. Each of your careers will see major upheavals driven by technology and globalization. Through all of this there are two abilities that will be your best friends – the ability to keep learning (and unlearning) and the ability to develop resilience. Start developing these early and you will be rewarded for your focus.

Through it all, remember how personal careers really are. Everyone's trajectory is unique. Both the authors share our own stories through this volume and speak about how each one of us has handled the crossroads of our careers differently. Your career is an important part of your life and what makes your career satisfying (or not) is how well its flow matches your internal rhythm, your personal priorities, your passion. We have met many outwardly successful people who in fact are quite miserable on the inside.

Always remember – the most satisfying careers are designed and not just achieved.

Designing your career (and your life) requires you to keep paying attention to what kind of work energizes and engages you and then design your life around that. Work, at its best, can transport you to a beautiful place of complete peace where time practically stands still, and you are in complete harmony with yourself.

It exists. We have been there. We hope you find it too.

one

UNDERSTAND

Just as different people have their own personalities, organizations have unique personalities too. They are varied in the ways they think, solve problems and make decisions. These peculiarities are part of their distinct culture.

1

ICEBERG TIPS AND UNSEEN BLIPS

Twenty-five years ago, when I (Shalini) graduated from business school, I skipped the popular, and safe, campus placement process to find a job on my own. I had just finished working on a year-long internship in Delhi and was looking for a job in Bengaluru where my then-fiancé lived.

Having just finished a stint assisting a leading consultant in interpersonal dynamics, I pondered over my criteria for deciding what would be a good place to work. I wanted to work with an organization where people were happy. Since email was not yet commonly used, it was normal to take printouts of your résumé and hand it over at the reception of an organization with a request that it reach the Human Resources (HR) department.

This meant personal visits to the offices of potential employers. Often, while I waited at the reception, I had the opportunity to watch people come into office in the morning. This made for some interesting viewing. At some organizations, people walked in with ease and greeted each other with warmth, while at others, people walked in looking very serious and seemed rather unhappy to be there. I was hoping to join an organization with a warm and friendly atmosphere and the time I spent at the reception watching people told me that I had finally found the right place for me when I reached Titan Industries.

Although I wasn't smart enough to know what I was doing back then, it turns out that I had stumbled upon the *corporate iceberg.* The corporate iceberg refers to the many layers of beliefs that comprise an organization's culture. What is visible to the casual observer (policies, structures) is a tiny fraction of what an organization really stands for. But if you know what you are really looking at and understand that there are a lot of factors and influences in every organization that are not apparent at first glance, you can find your way around any organization in just a short time. Indeed, small observations can, in fact, tell you much about what has made the organization what it is.

In this chapter we will share with you what an organization's culture is, how important it is and how you can understand it. We will share with you several secrets to 'decode' your organization's culture. While there is no end to this decoding, we will help you get started. Gradually, you will learn to see far beyond what is apparent, and develop a deeper understanding of the world you have entered.

'Culture eats strategy for breakfast'

An important way to understand an organization is by studying its culture. The remark 'culture eats strategy for breakfast', attributed to famous management thinker Peter Drucker emphasizes the point. We have often heard the term 'culture' being used to denote whether an organization is easy or difficult to work in. But the concept of culture is actually far deeper and more layered than just being a term to describe how easy it is to work at a place.

The concept of organizational culture was developed by organizational scholar Edgar Schein to explain why and how larger work groups like organizations behave the way they do. While many definitions of culture exist, Schein himself offers one of the most comprehensive definitions of culture when he says:

> It is a pattern of basic assumptions invented, discovered or developed by a given group as it learns to cope with its problems of external adaptation and internal integration that has worked well enough to be considered valid and therefore is taught to new members as the correct way to perceive, think and feel in relation to those problems (Schein 1988).[1]

Although it sounds a bit academic, this definition is a very valuable one. It first explains what culture is (a pattern of basic assumptions). Then it explains how and why culture develops (to cope with external adaptation and internal integration). Finally, it describes how culture gets passed on (as past solutions are taught to new members).

Why is understanding organizational culture so important? Everything an organization does is driven by its culture in ways that most employees are rarely conscious of. So, without understanding an organization's culture, you will keep bumping into invisible walls every time you try something that is not supported by it. And this will not make any sense to you. Most people in an organization think in terms of a strategy – a logical method and approach. Culture, on the other hand, is human, vulnerable, emotional and volatile. Even the most well-thought-through strategy will fail if it doesn't take into account this far more powerful force that is culture.

People who have been in an organization a long time may not be able to help you understand these invisible walls because over time, they may have internalized the organization's beliefs so deeply that the organization's traditional way seems the only logical way to do business. With the organization's beliefs and their own beliefs being so closely intertwined, they may not be able to step back and articulate the organization's culture – but they will act from it. There is an old saying that a fish is the last to be aware of the water. Well, the same is true of any culture. Stay long enough and all the peculiar beliefs of your organization will begin to seem only too natural to you.

Levels of organizational culture

An organization's culture is often described as an iceberg. Just like an iceberg, which floats 10 per cent above water and 90 per cent underwater, most of an organization's culture is hidden from sight – it lies in the mental habits of its people. Unsurprisingly, there are many levels at which you can observe an organization's culture, ranging from the most visible to the least. This important idea, also introduced by Schein, is a very useful one for anyone who really wants to understand organizations.

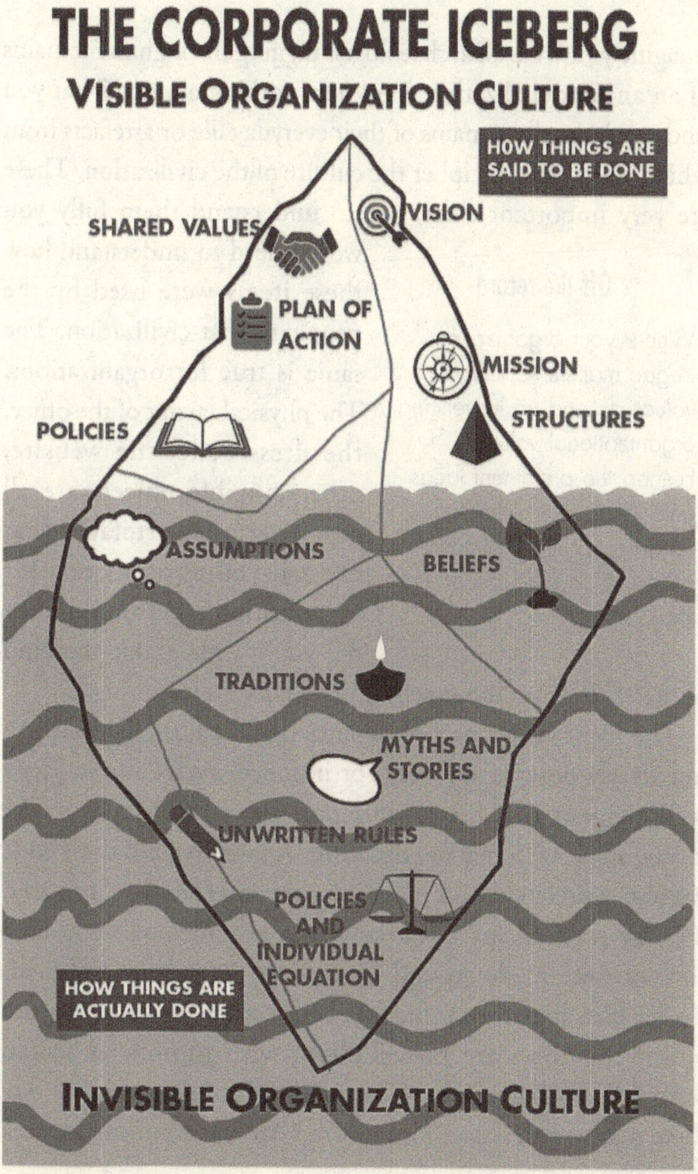
THE CORPORATE ICEBERG
VISIBLE ORGANIZATION CULTURE
HOW THINGS ARE SAID TO BE DONE
VISION
SHARED VALUES
PLAN OF ACTION
MISSION
POLICIES
STRUCTURES
ASSUMPTIONS
BELIEFS
TRADITIONS
MYTHS AND STORIES
UNWRITTEN RULES
POLICIES AND INDIVIDUAL EQUATION
HOW THINGS ARE ACTUALLY DONE
INVISIBLE ORGANIZATION CULTURE

Visible symbols of organizational culture (Artefacts)

Imagine you were an archaeologist digging through the remains of an ancient civilization you knew nothing about. What you find would be the remains of their everyday life or artefacts from which you would decipher the culture of the civilization. These are very important clues, but to understand them fully you would need to understand how these items were used by the people of that civilization. The same is true for organizations. The physical layout of the office, the dress code, the website, other tangible objects are all organizational artefacts that can tell you a lot about your organization's culture as they tell you a little about the kind of beliefs that set these behaviours and systems in place.

Off the record

Where your organization began matters. Country values do end up influencing organizational values. Further, the prominent ideas and values at the time your organization was founded often live on even decades later.

The most visible part of organizational culture is what you can clearly observe and see. For instance, a very formal dress code suggests that the organization views business as a very formal space with marked decorum. A more relaxed dress code suggests a preference for more informal interactions. Similarly, the way physical space is arranged in an office tells you how choices were made around how power is to be distributed. To see how hierarchy influences office space, observe whether senior members are placed along with juniors or seated separately. What kinds of interactions are encouraged? Are there many open spaces for meeting? Are there informal spaces where employees can simply relax? Each of these elements is an outcome of choices made by the organization and reveals its values.

> There are other subtle visible clues you can pick up about an organization's culture. These are hidden in the way the organization is designed – how many layers of hierarchy are present and where do those in positions of power sit? You can also see these clues in the several documents produced for external audience such as brochures and annual reports, etc. Each document gives us insights about what the organization really values as it is the outcome of decisions made based on what was considered important by the company.
>
> Today, most organizations try to have a strong presence online. The company website or other social media pages reveal what the organization considers important information to communicate about itself.

Espoused beliefs

These refer to consciously articulated statements around what an organization values, but can also be in the form of stated strategies or philosophies. In many cases, these represent what the organization would like to believe, but may not be the same as its actual beliefs. In fact, as many management thinkers have observed, it is rare for the espoused beliefs and actual beliefs to be the same.

Most organizational meetings and discussions take place around espoused beliefs. If an organization's conscious articulation of its beliefs is very different from the beliefs it actually lives by, you may find the organization operating in deep confusion.

Now unless you are an astute observer, you could work for an organization for a long time before realizing the many different layers through which its culture operates. You might be tempted to naïvely believe the stated values without critical examination or you may feel disappointed when the organization fails to live up to its stated beliefs. For instance, you may find yourself in an organization that insists it makes decisions democratically (stated belief) while in reality it is constantly making decisions that are top-down in its approach.

Remember, organizations are, after all, human collectives and therefore face challenges just like we do at actually being its ideal version. Each of us may have a vision of our 'best self' or the kind of person we would like to be. Our daily actions may or may not however be completely consistent with this vision of ourselves. Similarly, organizations may state in their vision statements that they believe in something but actually struggle to live by those beliefs each day. Despite these difficulties, stated beliefs are helpful because they help you understand what the organization aspires to be, or at least how it would like others to think of it.

Underlying assumptions

Remember Schein's definition of organizational culture as a set of underlying basic assumptions that are developed by an organization as it seeks to find solutions to its everyday challenges? Let's see how we can use this definition to understand how an organization's culture develops.

Imagine that you and a friend start a business. Initially, you will make many decisions about your operations: what kind of business you want to start, who your customers will be, how they will become your customers, how you will engage with them, etc. You will also need to decide what kind of people you hire first, how they will be paid, how work will be divided, how you will interact with each other, and so on. Now each of these decisions could be made in many different ways. And your underlying assumptions of who would be a good employee and what would be a good way to retain or motivate them will guide the choices you make. Note that you may not be even consciously thinking about culture just as yet but you are already influencing it through these very routine operational decisions.

Off the record

A great way to understand an organization's culture is to understand what kind of people are really successful there.

As you grow and remain in business, you will need to make many more seemingly routine decisions. You will set the ground rules for what your organization will and will not do. You will need to resolve conflicts within and outside the organization. If you are in a situation where you are cheated by another party or have been asked for a bribe, you will need to decide how you will respond.

As you begin to find your answers to each of these operational challenges, you will continue to make choices at every step of the way. As you do, you will develop some preferred ways of resolving dilemmas. Some of your choices will be conscious and others will simply be an expression of how you naturally make decisions. Consciously or not, you have now set the foundation for your organization's culture.

When the company you now work at began, its founders also needed to make many routine decisions. And each time they found something that worked well, they quite likely repeated, and soon instituted, the action. Hence, at the foundation of your organization's culture is a set of unquestioned rules and assumptions about its values and beliefs around the work done, how people should be treated, how problems should be solved, and so on. Each of these values are continuously layered through the hundreds of small operational decisions made each day. These are the invisible yet powerful roots to your organization's culture.

As you may have guessed from this example, the values of the people who start the organization or those who lead it in the early years play a very important role in shaping the culture of the organization. This is known as the founders' blueprint.[2]

The founders' blueprint

Over a hundred years ago, this letter marked the start of one of India's most prestigious colleges, the Indian Institute of Science.

Esplanade House, Bombay
Nov. 23 1898

Dear Swami Vivekananda

I trust you remember me as a fellow-traveller on your voyage from Japan to Chicago. I very much recall at this moment your views on the growth of the ascetic spirit in India, and the duty, not of destroying, but of diverting it into useful channels.

I recall these ideas in connection with my scheme of the Research Institute of Science for India, of which you have doubtless heard or read. It seems to me that no better use can be made of the ascetic spirit than the establishment of monasteries or residential halls for men dominated by this spirit, where they should live with ordinary decency, and devote their lives to the cultivation of sciences – natural and humanistic. I am of opinion that if such a crusade in favour of an asceticism of this kind were undertaken by a competent leader, it would greatly help asceticism, science, and the good name of our common country; and I know not who would make a more fitting general of such a campaign than Vivekananda.

Do you think you would care to apply yourself to this mission of galvanising into life our ancient traditions in this respect? Perhaps, you had better begin with a fiery pamphlet rousing our people in this matter. I would cheerfully defray all the expenses of publication.

With kind regards,

I am, dear Swami,
Yours faithfully,
Jamsetji N. Tata

This letter from one legendary thinker to another tells you all you need to know of the intention with which the institute was set up. If you are still curious, you can read up about Jamsetji Tata, his values and beliefs, and those of the early leaders of the institute. Knowing the values of the people who founded an institution will help you understand the way in which critical choices were made in the early years of an organization. Thus, as we shall see in the example below, the founders of any organization create a blueprint that is followed for a long, long time.

The Founders' Blueprint in Action

A decade ago, when at a programme for DuPont in Goa, I (Shalini) learnt that employees were not allowed to travel on a motorbike in the evening because of safety concerns. Very curious about this precaution, I dug deeper.

It turns out that DuPont was set up on money made through the trade of gunpowder. As you can imagine, transporting gunpowder 200 years ago would have required an organization to be extra careful about safety.

Now, in a display of the tremendous tenacity of a founder's blueprint, this emphasis on safety had become so internalized that hundreds of years later, in a beach town in India, it influenced transport decisions. This is an example of how subtly and yet deeply a founder's blueprint influences an organization's decisions even a hundred years later.

The founders' blueprint is often unstated, and it is, therefore, even more powerful. The personality of the founder(s), their values and their fundamental outlook on work and life contribute to a schema of mental maps that becomes part of an organization's culture.

Interestingly, research has shown that the founders' blueprint is so hardwired into the culture of an organization that it is very difficult to untangle it even decades after the company has been functional. In fact, organizations that attempt transformations without paying attention to their founders' blueprint have often found themselves struggling with change.

Sometimes, when the founder of an organization is a public figure and has a larger-than-life personality – like Steve Jobs – their impact on the organization is easy to understand.

However, there are many other founders who have not been in the public eye and have less prominent personalities. Their values and beliefs, and hence their influence, may not be very obvious. If that is the case with your organization, you may want to dig a bit deeper and search for any early stories (or even myths) about your founder(s). In the following chapter, we will share how stories are a great way to understand your organization.

Tips and Takeaways

- You will be better fit for some work cultures more than others. Knowing this can be quite liberating because adjusting to a new place of work is not just about you fitting in; it is about your organization being the right fit for you too.
- There are clues of culture everywhere. Today, your first set of clues will be online. Who are the senior leaders? What do they say? What does their website say? What vibe does it communicate? What do customers and employees say about the company?
- Once you join an organization, your observation skills are your best friend. There are clues everywhere that reflect the organization's values and beliefs. Observe how meetings are conducted, what is discussed and how decisions are made. Each of these reveals the deepest values of the organization.
- Use your understanding of your organization's culture to think through how to be most effective within the organization.

2

MYTHS IN OUR MIDST

Who doesn't love a good story? We know we do! As you spend time in your organization, you'll find that listening to its stories is a great way to understand its culture. We know that an organization's culture is multi-layered – there are parts that everyone speaks about and is familiar with, and then there are parts that are lived every day but rarely acknowledged.

One instance where the richness of an organization's culture comes together in a neat package is during talks regarding the past of the organization. Often overlooked, an organization's stories are an important source of learning about what your organization really values. In this chapter, we will talk about how to seek and understand what these stories say about your organization.

Organizational mythology

Every culture has its own set of myths and legends, and they communicate a way to understand the world and what is important in it. Before humans learnt to write, they told stories. These were tales of heroes and villains, of jealousy and arrogance, of courage and conviction. Early humans narrated their tales to carry forward their understanding of the world and their values. The tapestry of an organization's stories is called its mythology. You might have encountered the term mythology when talking about a society's mythic past, like Greek, Roman or Indian mythology. These often-fantastical stories with characters that capture our imagination teach us important lessons. Mythology shows people how the heroes of their culture resolved the dilemmas of life, providing guideposts for regular people as they navigate similar dilemmas. By capturing the imagination, mythology is often far more powerful than many other narrations that are rooted in historical facts.

Off the record

Keep an ear out for the stories being told. It's not just gossip – it's research.

Organizations also have stories that form their mythology, which communicate to the listener what the organization holds dear. Some of these stories may date back to the early days of the organization and demonstrate how a key founder resolved a dilemma. Other stories may be more recent and will tell you about how the organization dealt with a contemporary issue.

Pay attention to these stories, because even if you feel that it is idle gossip, it is not. The stories are a part of your learning about the organization. And they are likely to give you clues about the hidden aspects that influence behaviour in your organization. Unlike the fantastical stories of the great mythologies, organizational mythology is dressed rather plainly. It is powerful, but in a very quiet and discreet way.

So what does an organization's mythology look like? Researchers who study organizational mythology find that stories that speak to the common dilemmas people face are popularly sought out.

The stories in your organization will be unique to it, yet you will find that there are certain common elements that run deep in organizations, no matter which industry you are a part of. We hope that when you read these stories presented below, you will be able to spot and interpret the stories you have encountered.

Story type 1: How much do employees care about the organization?

Ten years ago, after joining as HR head in a traditional manufacturing organization, the induction included meeting people across the organization in small focus groups to understand their experience of working with the firm. One story was repeated often.

It turned out that at the height of a particularly difficult time for the business, the group ran out of money to pay salaries at the organization. Many people had been with the organization a long time and chose to remain with it through thick and thin. Though the salaries stopped, they continued working. They borrowed money wherever they could and soldiered on. Some months later the company was able to finally pay their accumulated salaries. In essence, the average employee bailed out the company in its moment of need.

This story had a strong impact on everyone who heard it – both, employees who had worked in the firm during those days and the new entrants. It illustrated the relationship the employees had with the organization – one of deep personal commitment. The episode mentioned reflected a time of distress for the company and those who had worked there. This single story that was passed on to all new employees was more effective in conveying the standard of work and commitment that was expected by the company than any induction speech that could have been given.

Off the record

The stories old-timers tell you are gold. They reveal the critical 'culture-making' moments.

Story type 2: Is the boss human?

Hierarchies are drilled into us from a young age and we often carry those perceptions to work as well. All of us wonder whether our bosses or senior executives can cross the divide that hierarchy sets up and work along with us. An approachable boss is easy to work with, will ensure that every employee feels like they are heard and look to involve them in decision-making. This next story deals with one such incident.

> In 2001, I had joined as a consultant at a leading HR Consulting firm. The organization was based out of Chennai, while I lived in Delhi. Soon after I joined, I needed to travel to Chennai to attend an important day-long discussion regarding a new project. My flight got a bit delayed and by the time I reached the meeting the team was deep in discussion. Most of the people in the room were unfamiliar. I only recognized the business head who had interviewed me and a college professor I knew from long back. The discussions were very intense and I was rather vocal – far more than would be considered appropriate

> for the first day of work. In my defence, I was extremely passionate about the topic.
>
> One of the persons I disagreed with often enough was a colleague who was equally passionate. He had given me a warm handshake and introduced himself by his nickname right when I entered, but other than that I had no idea what his role was.
>
> Later, during the tea break I asked my hiring manager whether I would get an opportunity to meet the founder and CEO. Puzzled, he explained that I just had. It was of course the very same colleague I had been arguing with. Somewhat concerned, I went up to him and apologized. He just laughed warmly, and our difference of opinion was never an issue between us. At that moment I knew I was in the right place for me.

More than any values statement on a company wall, this one story captures the essence of how an organization should be considerate about the opinions of every employee. The way hierarchy plays out in meetings, how disagreements with the big boss impact you and how open and honest discussions can be is a good marker of how much a company will encourage your growth.

Story type 3: What happens when the organization gets into trouble?

One common, yet mostly unexpressed, worry for an employee is whether the organization is a stable place to work. We all wonder whether we are working for the kind of organization that is quick to lay-off its employees when business is not doing well. And we worry about whether such layoffs will be humane or will leave us high and dry. Take this one story shared by a former colleague who worked at Lehman Brothers right till the end in 2008.

> Many people ask me if I had known what was happening, right at the end. And I tell them very honestly that I did not, even though I was working in New York City right in the headquarters, and was a vice president at Lehman Brothers in September 2008.
>
> Just a few weeks before the end, our CEO gave a public address to all the employees. 'Every one of you should feel confident and proud. Our firm is strong today. And we will emerge from this cycle even stronger. We've done it before and we will do it again.' We listened to him and then went on with our business.
>
> Some of our friends on the outside were calling us asking if we had any inside news on the company – we said we didn't actually have any. In fact we were working on a major project presentation for all the days leading right up to the end. I only began to get worried when, about 24 hours before the announcement of bankruptcy, I just couldn't reach my boss. That was very unusual and it got me worried. We got to know about the bankruptcy filing the same day the outside world did.

Stories like this are likely to be told and retold in an organization to emphasize the fact that anything can happen to the business in a fashion peculiar to every industry, when you least expect it. In this case, the organization has ceased operation, but the stories live on, regardless, as cautionary tales of signs to look out for.

Story type 4: Can the little person rise to the top?

This story deals with internal mobility and the fundamental question of the possibilities for individual growth within an organization. Not surprisingly, this story plays into the question each of us has for ourselves – if we stay here, can we reach the top? If the environment in your organization allows for a large amount of mobility and growth, you will very likely hear of it through stories such as these.

> **Off the record**
>
> In some organizations it is the negative stories that are really popular. If so, you are working for an organization with a demoralized and cynical workforce. This is not a healthy sign.

This is a story from an Indian organization that highlights how these play out.

> Once, when conducting focus groups among young employees at a well-known clean energy organization to understand what they liked about working there, I was struck by the enthusiasm and energy of the groups. I asked them how they felt about the organization and a common refrain was that they felt very hopeful about their own careers here because they had seen deserving people do extremely well.
>
> The one story that was repeated in several of these focus groups was the story of Raghavan, a very bright and talented engineer who had joined the organization eight years before, straight out of college. As the organization grew, he grew with it. That day, at just 28, he was the head of a very critical function. Not only was Raghavan very smart, he was also level-headed and a great mentor to young people. When people joined the organization, they

> looked at Raghavan's position and felt inspired and hopeful about their own careers.

Raghavan's story ensured that when young people joined the organization, they felt they had made the right choice. They felt that as long as they were competent and prepared to work very hard, the organization would give them all the opportunities they sought, and this motivated them greatly.

Story type 5: Will the organization help me in my time of need?

A type of organizational story that is particularly popular in India studies incidents where an employee is going through a difficult time in his/her personal life and then follows how (and if) the organization found a way to respond and support the employee. Take, for example, this episode a former colleague went through:

> **Off the record**
>
> Often the positive stories in an organization are anchored around the actions of just a few key people. It suggests that this is the kind of organization that allows good people to thrive.

> My daughter was diagnosed with cancer just two months after I had joined a new organization, and my whole life changed. As she was in and out of hospitals, I was very worried about the impact this was going to have on my new job. However, to my delight, the managing director (MD) connected me to the head of Rajiv Gandhi Cancer Institute in Delhi, where her treatment finally took place. The MD was concerned and understanding about all the time I needed to take off. It really reaffirmed my faith in the organization.

Many older Indian organizations are very good at helping employees in their time of need. By helping one employee, they give many other employees who are observing the situation the confidence that they are working for a 'good organization' – one that will be there for them in times of need.

Story type 6: How will the boss react to a mistake?

We all worry about what will happen to us when we make an honest mistake. We worry about whether the organization will be harsh or lenient with us. Perhaps that's why stories around how mistakes were dealt with are so popular in an organization. This story was shared by a friend.

> My first job was as a training manager at a manufacturing company. Even before I joined the company, I had heard stories about my boss, Mandy (name changed), who was known as someone who really looked after her team. People said she was a coaching manager and wanted to see everyone on her team do well. Fresh from university, I was worried about making mistakes because I had a number of responsibilities and not a lot of experience in a large organization. People told me not to worry because Mandy would always stand by me.
>
> Where I worked, we had an organization, Alliance, that was jointly funded by the union and the management. It focused on imparting life skills to our employees, who were union members. Mandy nominated me to be part of the curriculum team of Alliance. I was excited to join the team and was full of ideas. In one of the meetings, with all innocent enthusiasm, I made many recommendations on

what we could do differently. I thought I was being very creative and thinking out of the box. What I hadn't realized was that in my presentation I had also been very critical about many current practices in the company.

This was a big mistake not because there was no room for improvement but because of the manner in which I made my case. I later found out that the head of Alliance had gone to Mandy and told her in no uncertain terms that they didn't want me on the team any more.

Fortunately, Mandy believed in giving people a fair chance and stood by her team. She believed that I would bring a lot of value and new ideas to the group and wanted me to be a part of the team there. She helped me understand my mistake and coached me on my communication style. She also did not back down and convinced the head of Alliance to give me a second chance.

As a result, I adapted my communication style, built good working relationships with most of the people in that organization, and even managed to get some of my ideas implemented.

Story type 7: How will the organization deal with obstacles?

There are perhaps few stories as powerful as the ones that speak of the tremendous heroism displayed by many during the terrorist attacks on the Taj Mahal Palace hotel in Mumbai in November 2008. 'The Ordinary Heroes of the Taj', an article in the *Harvard Business Review*, poignantly recounts the bravery, values and ethics of employees of the Taj Mahal Palace hotel.[1] Let's look at how general manager Karambir Singh Kang reacted during the attack.

> Kang was at a conference away from the hotel when he heard about the attacks. He returned immediately and took charge of the situation, overseeing the evacuation of guests and assisting the firefighters despite the general confusion and panic. He thought that his family would be safe in the general manager's suite on the sixth floor and asked them to stay locked in their rooms. However, he soon realized that the terrorists were on the upper floors and so tried to reach his family. It was an effort doomed to fail because of the constant exchange of gunfire between the terrorists and the army. Soon, the sixth floor was engulfed in flames, and there was no hope of anyone surviving the inferno.
>
> Despite what must have been unbearable grief and pain, Kang worked tirelessly to lead the rescue efforts. He only called his family the next day to let them know that his wife and children had perished in the attack. Even though he could have asked for a transfer to any other Taj property across the world, Kang stayed on at the Taj and was an integral part of the team that led the restoration of this iconic hotel.

Stories like these powerfully communicate the personal courage of the employees. They show how senior management at the hotel have reacted in times of crisis, and just how much guests are valued at the Taj. A single powerful story is enough to convey and propagate an organization's culture for a long time to come and to people in any other location.

The last story is one that deals with a temptation that we are all susceptible to, no matter where you are in the hierarchy of the organization: how to deal with bribery.

Story type 8: Will the organization pay bribes to get its work done?

If you work for an organization that prides itself on its ethics, chances are that they will have a somewhat apocryphal story around bribes. These stories are particularly popular in India because the telling and retelling helps members of the organization resolve an important dilemma in their minds: will we pay or take bribes if needed?

The following story was shared by the founder of a very successful energy organization:

> When I had just started working, I was warned by all my relatives that I was being too naïve. They told me that doing business in India was nothing like doing business in the United States. Since so much of our work comes from the government, they told me that there was no way I could do business without bribes.
>
> But I was determined to create a successful business without paying bribes. Since we were in the energy business, we needed permissions for using land to set up solar farms. The very first time our papers got stuck in a government office, I personally went over and parked myself at the government office. I was at their office from 9 a.m. to 5 p.m., and each time an officer would step out, I would ask him about my papers.
>
> Now, they could see that I was well-educated and looked like a professional. I told them all about the work I did in the United States, and the political leaders who had encouraged me. Eventually, perhaps they realized that it was just easier for them to pass my papers and get rid of me, or perhaps concerned about any higher-ups that I might be connected

> with, and approved my papers. Later, the IAS officer who oversaw the department became a friend of mine. He was very impressed by my persistence and the fact that I just wanted to do good for the country. I find that if you are persistent and thorough with your paperwork, it may take you longer, but your work will be done without bribing anyone.

Now it is likely that as this story gets shared across the organization, it becomes an important transmitter of organizational values. Next time someone else working for the organization has files stuck in an office, they will not rush to pay bribes. These are the kinds of stories that over time have a big impact on an organization's culture.

Discovering your organization's stories

So how do you begin finding out stories of your organization? Well, now that you know the framework to look out for and the kinds of stories you might hear, you can begin to consciously pay attention to what you hear at the office.

The first place you are likely to encounter interesting stories about your organization is at your induction programme. You might be told stories of critical incidents that reflect what the organization is most proud of. If you work for a well-established organization that has been in the public eye for a while, you may also find stories about the organization online or in books written about the organization. Listen to these stories carefully for they will tell you what the organization values.

What makes organizational mythology such a powerful transmitter of culture is that no one leader can fully control the narrative. People watch how leaders make choices in difficult situations and that becomes a story. In time, the story becomes part of the mythology shared by people across the organization. By its very nature this is a very democratic process. These stories are also very dynamic, continuously being reshaped by more recent events and experiences.

Now that we have spent all this time understanding what culture is (a set of shared assumptions about work) and how it gets revealed (observation and stories), we move on to a whole other lens to understand your organization – its business.

Tips and Takeaways

- Stories matter. They carry very important messages about how the organization makes choices at critical crossroads. Listen to them and reflect on what they reveal about the company.
- The most important stories in an organization will be the ones you hear time and again. With each retelling the message will be reinforced. This is one way culture is transmitted.
- An organization's stories are being created and recreated each day. In that sense it is the most up-to-date barometer for how people in an organization really feel about it.
- All stories of goodness in an organization are really about what people in the organization feel proud of. They reflect how the organization acts when it is at its best. Don't expect the organization to always live up to these high standards.
- At the end of the day, stories are very democratic. They are the interpretation given by observers to events important to them. This narrative is never completely controlled by the top brass.

3

THINK BUSINESS

In the previous chapters we looked at one powerful source of understanding your organization: its culture. In this chapter, we will look at another powerful way of understanding your organization: its business. What you do in order to create a profit in business (for commercial organizations) or to create an impact (for not-for-profit organizations) fundamentally affects the way your organization works. This is why all firms in a given industry share many similar features: work processes, organizational structures and even people practices.

What is most exciting about viewing your organization from the lens of its business is that it doesn't matter which part of the world you work in, and it doesn't matter what industry you are in. These questions are universal. As you begin to find your answers to them, you will understand what your organization is trying to do and why your organization works the way it does.

Once you understand the business of your organization, you will find that you have the ability to contribute to the organization more deeply. You will be able to see how your work connects with the larger concerns of the organization.

You will also be able to think of new ways to contribute that go beyond your job description. Finally, you will also be able to think of new initiatives for the organization.

We believe that there are five important questions that will help you quickly zero in on the central forces that influence your organization's business. If the search for answers feels a bit overwhelming in the beginning, do not worry. Understanding the questions is itself a great start. Once you have some basic understanding of the questions, begin to collect factual information. The questions in this chapter are different from the questions in the previous chapters. Much of this information may actually be in the public domain already or can easily be found out by speaking to someone in the strategy function, the sales and marketing function or the finance function. It is the piecing together of this information that is important, and the longer you are with an organization, the better you will understand the implications and nuances of it.

So what are these five questions and how did we arrive at them?

There are two important sources of these questions. The first source is a popular framework – the business canvas by a strategy consulting firm called Strategyzer.[1] While this framework was originally designed to enable business leaders to make good choices, we feel it is easy enough for anyone to use, regardless of designation. The second source is mentorship advice given to us by a few senior partners from leading global consulting firms. We asked them to share with us the questions they used to help new consultants understand their client's business. We are sharing these with you because we think they will equally help you understand your own organization.

We suggest that you keep these five questions handy and actively seek out conversations with people who can help answer these questions. Most organizations welcome such inquisitiveness from newcomers. It is an uncommon enough practice to mark you out as someone with a sharp and inquisitive mind. So go ahead, don't hesitate and ask somebody these questions. If on the other hand, you are working in an organization where asking questions is not quite encouraged, you may want to think of finding the answers as a jigsaw puzzle. Supplement the answers you find in the public domain by intelligent questions to help you fill in the blanks. Additionally, as you get to know the organization over a period of time, you will find your own ways to find people who are happy to explain their work to you.

1. What is the value that your organization is creating?

Stated simply, the value your organization creates is the reason why someone will be your customer. Sometimes, these reasons are simple and functional (for instance, a car gets you from point A to point B), and the need your product or service fulfils is a straightforward one. At other times, you may need to dig deeper to discover that the actual need that your product or service satisfies goes beyond its functionality.

To continue with the example of the car, while any car can get you from one point to another, driving in a luxury car may make people feel successful. Therefore, the value created by a company such as BMW is not just the functionality of helping you move around, but it includes the experience of luxury and

perhaps associated value of success. Most successful products or services provide a solution to one or more of a customer's needs. So, do you know why people buy your product? Not just the features of your product, but the problem the product solves for your customer? This is your value proposition.

To really understand how you create value, you must first understand who your customer really is. You may have many different kinds of customers, and each type of customer might have different needs that are being satisfied by your product or service. Your product development or marketing teams would be able to provide insights into these kinds of questions.

There are two other ways to understand how your organization fulfils your customer's needs. The first is to understand how your products or services actually reach the customer, or the distribution channels your organization uses. The second is to understand the nature of the relationship your organization has with its customers. Is it a one-time or sporadic engagement or do you have an ongoing and deep relationship? Each of these answers is a statement of how your organization has decided to interact with its customers.

> **Off the record**
>
> The industry and your organization's positioning within it often have huge implications on the kind of people that work there and its preferred ways of making decisions.

It is in fact likely that your organization has multiple ways of reaching customers. Your customers could buy your products online either through your own store or a vendor's online store? Or perhaps they could buy your products in a physical store too? Each of these represents a different distribution channel with a different dynamic and

process of interacting with the customer. Similarly, consider the nature of the relationship your organization has with its customers. Is it a relationship where you have multiple points of contact (think Uber or an airline) or is it a one-off relationship (like a real estate company)? Each of these questions are great places to begin understanding the value you create and how this value is delivered to your customer.

You will receive some of this information as part of your induction process. If your organization sells your product directly to the consumers, it is also likely that distribution and sales information will be available online. For any other questions you might have, one or two meetings with someone from the sales and marketing department should be able to fill up all the gaps.

Understand Your Customer

- Talk to your colleagues from sales and product development. Ask them to explain what the product does and what the customer looks for in it.
- Wherever possible, visit a customer. If it is not always possible, make a special request to do so. You could also design a project that will give you access to customers.
- If you work in an industry that sells products to people like you (FMCG or electronic goods), drop into stores that stock your products and observe/talk to people.

2. How is this value created?

The next step is to understand how value for your product actually gets created. In other words, how does your

organization structure itself to consistently deliver its products and services?

If you are a manufacturing organization, this may mean understanding the manufacturing processes and other functions like research and development (R&D), supply chain, purchase, and so on. If you are in a service organization, this would mean getting into the many aspects of service operations. While it is not important to know all the details about the operations of the organization, it helps to have at least a broad idea of how your products or services are created.

A good starting point to understand how your organization creates value is to understand the key activities within its operations. Looking at the organizational chart will help you ask specific questions about the role of different teams and how they integrate to create the product. Start right at the top while reading an organizational chart. Observe which roles report to the CEO. Each of these roles is likely to have a unit under them. Understanding how each unit's work connects with other units will help you understand how value is created in your organization. Once you understand how value is created at the very top of the organization, you can work your way down a few levels for a deeper understanding.

Going back to our example of the car manufacturing company, you are likely to see these functions report to your CEO: Sales and marketing, Finance, HR, Operations, information technology (IT) and R&D. On close observation, you will be able to see the role that each of these functions plays in making the car and getting it to the customer. For example, R&D comes up with the design and technical specifications for the car which is then manufactured by Operations. Once the cars are made, Sales and Marketing are responsible for creating awareness about the car and getting it into all the company-authorized dealerships across the country. Finance, HR and IT are support functions that help all the other functions do their jobs. At the surface level, you now have a sense of how your organization arranges itself to deliver its products. Using organizational charts as a starting point to understanding your organization is a simple way to delve deeper and ask questions around how work is organized. You may find that most people are quite happy to share what they do, and you may want to use every opportunity you get to understand their work till you are able to connect the dots yourself.

Off the record

An organizational chart is a shorthand for the way work is organized there.

Each business requires a set of key resources in order to be able to consistently deliver on its promise to its customer. Understanding these key resources is another source of insights into what's most important to keep your business running. For our car manufacturer, critical resources may include hard-to-source yet essential components, or great product design or state-of-the-art production facilities.

Understand Operations

- Look at the organizational structure of your company. Work tends to be clustered around teams, and understanding what each team does will help you understand what the main activities of your company are.
- Talk to a colleague from operations to understand the flow of work across different teams. Ask questions about who the key suppliers or strategic partners are.
- If you have the opportunity to speak to someone senior, ask them what they think are the most critical building blocks for your organization's operations.

You can ask one final set of questions to gain a deeper understanding of how your organization creates value: who are your partners in the process of creating value? These partners could be key suppliers or those who provide components critical to your business. They could be strategic alliances or partnerships. For a car manufacturer, this could be a key technology partner, suppliers of windscreens and tyres or even a product design company. Depending on the nature of your business, some operations may be outsourced. These outsourcing partners sometimes play a critical role in product or service delivery. The past few decades have seen outsourcing partnerships for operations or back-end jobs become a part of the way many large, global organizations operate.

3. How are you making money?

This question is at the very heart of running a business. How the organization earns money, how viable the business model is and how well it is doing financially compared to its peers are perhaps the most important questions for any organizational leader to answer to an organization's stakeholders.

As you start out in your career, thinking about your organization's financial health won't be your sole responsibility (was that a sigh of relief?). You will simply be assigned a role while your top leadership will be responsible for ensuring that the company is performing well. Many of us are quite happy with this limited responsibility. But if you are someone who wishes to rise up the organization and take on positions of higher responsibility, having a better idea of how the company makes money will help you prepare for leadership roles.

There are two main ways to assess how your organization makes money. The first is to understand how it generates its revenue. The second is to understand the costs that go into being able to deliver value. Both of these are connected to the two questions that we have already read about. Let's understand these concepts one by one.

Revenue streams

In question 1, we asked you to think about the value your organization creates and how it ensures that this value reaches its customers. Each customer or customer segment is a source of money for your business, also known as a revenue stream. If you are a multi-product, multi-segment organization, you are likely to have multiple revenue streams. These are simply different sources of income for the company. As we have already seen, you may have long-term, ongoing relationships with some of your customers, and you may have one-off relationships with others. Each of these relationships can be considered a revenue stream.

There are many other ways in which revenue streams flow in. You could be making income from product usage fees, licensing fees, leasing fees or subscription fees, and so on. As a result, any source of income for your organization is a revenue stream. Take the time to identify what the major revenue streams for your organization are. This will give you a very important insight into the priorities of the organization.

Cost structures

In question 2, we asked you to think about how your organization consistently delivers products or services. Each of the activities, resources and partnerships the company is engaged with point you to the costs of doing business in a particular way. The technical term for the particular way in which your organization chooses to deliver value to its customers and organize itself is called its business model.

Armed with this understanding of revenue streams and cost structures, you can now begin to see the key factors that determine the financial health of your organization. You might be surprised to hear that even very experienced business leaders find the process of managing the financial health of an organization challenging, although that is, in fact, their primary job.

Quite naturally, your business's viability depends on how much your revenue streams exceed your cost structures. If you are working for a public limited company (one that is traded on a stock exchange), this information will need to be published every financial quarter. While this is high-level data, it does give you an indication of how your organization is doing. Trends in a company's stock prices give you an indication of the market's overall confidence in its financial future.

However, you must remember that the stock market is not a very reliable indicator and is influenced by a number of factors outside the scope of our discussion. But here's an insider tip – the metrics that a company chooses to focus on can vary quite a bit. Given that there are many different financial metrics that are important, different leaders will most likely emphasize on different metrics. These metrics are usually very important indicators of what your organization cares about the most. Note what metrics are given greater priority in company meetings. Is it the EBITDA (Earnings before tax, depreciation and amortization – a term for operational profit)? Or is it the total revenue (money generated primarily through sales)? Or does the top management care about market leadership or market share (the percentage of the market controlled by the organization)? Each of these metrics suggests a different emphasis and is very useful while understanding what your organization values most.

Build financial literacy

Financial literacy is an understanding of how money is made, spent and saved. At its basic level, it constitutes a familiarity with some terms used by organizations to describe how money is being earned, spent or saved. There are many ways in which you can build your own financial literacy even if you did not go to business school (or did not focus on these courses when they were being taught!). We recommended three books on building this core skill in the notes at the end of this book, including a classic by Ben Graham.[2] You can also expand your financial literacy by taking 'finance for non-finance' courses. These are always some of the most popular courses offered in any executive education programme. Of course, you really do not need to go anywhere far – there are many good online courses that can get you started.

4. What industry are you in, how is it structured, and how are organizations in it structured?

The industry your organization operates in influences it more than might be apparent at first glance. Organizations within an industry tend to organize themselves rather similarly.

How they are organized reflects the dominant logic of market forces at a particular time. And this gets further amplified as different organizations in the same industry borrow practices from each other, recruit from each other and learn from each other. Over time, organizations in an industry tend to have much in common with each other.

For instance, the FMCG (fast-moving consumer goods) industry (which produces and sells most of your household products such as soaps, shampoos, cleaning solutions, etc.) has traditionally relied on strong marketing campaigns followed by widespread product availability. Organizations in this industry invest large amounts of money on advertising campaigns and then rely on a huge army of sales staff to ensure that their products are available in every nook and cranny of the country. None of this can be done without spending a considerable amount of money, and there are vast economies of scale, and barriers to entry for small players. As a result, the

FMCG industry is dominated by large global players and large Indian players – think Procter & Gamble, Reckitt Benckiser, Hindustan Unilever, Johnson & Johnson or Nestlé. These large organizations often have great systems, excellent marketing practices and efficient sales teams. They recruit management staff from top business schools and also spend a great deal on developing internal talent. The dynamics of this industry are, for instance, absolutely different from say the tech start-up space, which is dominated by several very small companies. The barriers to entry are relatively surmountable, and new entrepreneurs can create great value for customers in just a few years.

However, it is more likely that there will be more volatility within these small start-ups, and that through the early stages of their development they will operate through tremendous uncertainty. This means that there are few systems in place and that progress is likely to not be linear. In their early stages, the sole focus of these companies is on finding the right product-market fit. They have neither the resources nor the inclination to invest large amounts of money in talent development. Once these start-ups show promise, they often get funded or bought out by big players who can use their tremendous resources to help the concept behind the start-up come to life. You will find great talent in these organizations, but it is often limited to the founders or other team members with a stake in the company. It is only when these start-ups reach a certain size, scale and revenue that they begin to consciously think of talent development and other systems and processes. Think of how Flipkart, MakeMyTrip, Naukri.com, Myntra, Swiggy, Zomato and others grew.

To get an insight into how your industry works, you should

first see how business leaders have defined the boundaries of the industry. Then, research the different players (companies) in your industry. Next, try and understand how the sales within the industry are divided. Are they very fragmented (many small players)? Or is the market relatively consolidated (with a few fairly large players)? Who are the market leaders? Where is your organization vis-à-vis its competitors?

It is important to know how your industry is organized while trying to understand the way your firm behaves. For instance, if your organization is one player in a market dominated by a handful of players and with high barriers to entry, it is likely that you will have great commercial success. On the other hand, if you work for an organization in an industry with several other players and with no particular competitive advantage, the chances are that your profitability is hard won through internal efficiencies.

You also need to figure out the appeal you hold for customers compared to other organizations. This could be because of any one of these factors: superior brand appeal, superior product, widespread dealer network, great product styling, very efficient production, owning the network, etc. Try to understand how your organization's advantages compare with other organizations. This will give you key insights into what is at the heart of your organization's success within this industry – in essence, into its core competency.

If all this information seems like a lot, break it down into small portions. You could also treat it like a project and partner up with a few like-minded colleagues to join the different pieces together. As always, you can speak with senior colleagues in the marketing or strategy functions for more information. You could write out your questions before you talk to someone in these functions.

5. What is the impact of government and regulation on your industry?

Some industries are highly regulated by government norms, while others are relatively unregulated. Depending on which industry you are working in, government or regulatory authorities have a huge impact on your business. For instance, if you work for a financial services company, you will find that there are RBI guidelines to follow for every critical part of the business. These guidelines are intended to safeguard the interests of the customers and influence what your organization can or cannot do.

When working for a global financial institution, it was quite surprising to learn that everything initiated, even in talent and development, needed to be viewed through the lens of global regulators. Therefore, the leadership development programmes, the succession planning processes and other talent development processes had to be justifiable to external stakeholders. In case you are wondering, this is rather uncommon. On the other hand, if you are working for a small consulting company, the government has very little to say about your products or services, and you have a great degree of flexibility. You can, for instance, hire whoever you like in your company, you can offer your clients any kind of programme they may be interested in, and you can organize yourself in whichever way you find efficient without needing to check in with any government agency. Some great relief there!

Understanding your business may take some effort, but trust us, this effort will pay rich dividends. You may soon discover that you are able to make very valuable contributions at meetings, because unlike others you can see how the work of the organization is interconnected, and can express how you can contribute the most.

And as you gain more experience, your ability to see the business in its entirety will enable you to make strategic contributions, and this will help your chances in a talent or promotion discussion. Once you really understand the business, you will be well on your way to developing the business acumen that is so valued right at the top.

Understanding your organization's culture and its business gives you a solid foundation for learning how to navigate your organization – the focus of the next section.

Tips and Takeaways

- Set up a Google alert for your industry. This will keep you updated on important news related to your industry and help you understand the important forces behind its growth.
- Request senior colleagues in a few key functions to talk to you and help you understand the business. Nothing beats understanding your organization from the perspective of people in key functions.
- Visit customers or dealers. Speak to them about why they buy your product or service. This is the best way to understand the value your organization is creating.
- Read and understand your company's financial statements. This will help you understand how well your organization is running its business.

two

NAVIGATE

No one in an organization is an island unto themselves. You will be working with others all the time. How effective you will be will depend on the quality of these relationships.

4

BUILDING TIES

We'd like you to meet Sneha (name changed), a young professional with a unique and interesting background. Born in India but raised in the US, she had worked in the US pharmaceutical industry for four years before enrolling at the Indian School of Business (ISB) in Hyderabad for their one-year accelerated business programme. When the course ended, she was recruited by a US-headquartered pharmaceutical company as part of a high-profile recruitment programme for their business in India. She was placed in a product marketing role, and armed with her degrees and her work experience, Sneha approached her work with a sense of confidence.

While she had many good ideas pertaining to product marketing in general, she quickly realized that she needed to know a lot more about how to make these ideas work in her new organization. Unfortunately, her boss had limited time to coach and mentor her. At first, she was reluctant to ask her peers for help. But then she realized that that approach was going to get her nowhere. Building relationships with her peers became one of the most critical skills she had to master within the first few months of her new job.

Working with her company-assigned development coach, Sneha drafted a development goal: 'Build strong, trusting relationships with my peers.' She decided to use the dual approach of asking for their help *and* contributing to their success with her knowledge and experience. And thus, over time, she built trust with her peers and also learnt from them. She volunteered for projects and offered to take the lead in areas that played to her strengths. At the same time, she asked for help or guidance in areas that were new to her. In less than six months, Sneha had established herself as a strong team player.

The question you must ask yourself is this: Do you see your peers as competitors or collaborators? Do your peers see you as a follower or a leader? These are some of the most important ideas that we will discuss in this chapter because as a future leader, it is important that you are able to both follow and lead your peers. There will be occasions for you to display leadership qualities, and there will be times when teamwork should come first. You must be able to both cooperate and compete with your peers.

This chapter will discuss the importance of developing relationships with your peers in your team and in other teams. When you first join an organization fresh from college, you are teeming with enthusiasm and confidence. Your organization also wants you to channel these qualities and to contribute to your work. But very soon, you realize that you can get very little done on your own, and that you have to work with other people. As a result, good relationships within your team are essential in order to get work done.

Relationships with other teams are equally important because they will help you deepen your understanding of what your organization is working on. As you grow in your company, you will often need to work across teams. If you have already built relationships with some of these people, they will certainly help you get your work done. Of course, whenever you find like-minded people, you will be able to create friendships that can last a lifetime.

Giving and asking for help is the most natural form of give-and-take to build strong workplace relationships. When you have volunteered to help your colleagues with their work, especially in times when they are overworked, they too will be open to helping when you need it.

Give before you ask

During your first few days at a new job, you may not have a lot of work. However, there may be colleagues around you who have a full load of work and who may even be under a reasonable amount of stress because of it. A good way to start building relationships with your peers is to offer them help with their work. When you are seen as someone who is open to sharing, supporting others, they will also be ready and willing to help and support you in times of crisis.

This is exactly what Sneha did. She volunteered for work outside the definition of her role. In projects and tasks where she had some knowledge or prior experience, she even offered to take the lead without seeking recognition. Very quickly, she built a reputation as a trustworthy person because her peers found her reliable and competent even when she sought their help to do her own work.

Asking for help doesn't mean you are incompetent

Some of you may wonder: How can I ask for help? Won't people think I don't know my job? Will they think I'm incompetent? These fears usually keep us from asking for help. But remember, your peers were also once new to their roles and to the organization. They will remember what it was like when they were new, how lost they felt and are likely to help if you ask for it. When you ask for help, you should first do your homework and tackle the task as best you can. Once people see that you work hard, take the initiative and try creating your own solutions, they will be far more willing to help you.

Your peers are less likely to help if they think you are a shirker or someone who will immediately ask for help as an easy way out. Relationships are built when you show vulnerability and are willing to ask for help. Asking for help demonstrates humility and respect for your more experienced colleagues. However, there may be times when you know something new or something more than what your senior colleagues know. Be mindful of your reaction in this situation so as to not come across as a know-it-all.

Balance leading and following

As a fresh graduate, there might be new theories and ways of operating that you learnt at college or business school that some of your colleagues may not be aware of. Organizations need and want new ideas. Don't hesitate to share your ideas and your thoughts. Don't be afraid to take a leadership role, to influence or to ask people to follow you. If you disagree with something or have a better idea, express it, but remain open to others' points of view. You can offer your ideas respectfully, encouraging participation and idea sharing.

The secret to long-term success is to lead when leadership is called for and to be equally open to following others when follower-ship is needed. Following others doesn't make you weak; it only strengthens the team. It also shows flexibility and openness to other people's ideas. Sometimes, someone else's ideas may be better than yours or likely to give better results. Or, there may be times when you have not had the time to think through a problem and others may have. As long as you are not being asked to do anything unethical or illegal, when you see a task or a course of action as one benefiting the team or the organization, be willing to follow and support your peers. Teamwork relies on both giving and getting, and if you wish to get support, you must learn to give support. You will find that this process may occur several times a day, with the same people or with different people.

> **Off the record**
>
> You agree too much, and people think you don't have independent ideas. If you disagree too much, you are termed as a difficult person to work with. Find your balance.

As you spend more time in an organization, you will gradually get to know the people you work with. Rather than waiting for relations to get built over time, you could accelerate the process by reaching out to others.

Get to know your team

When you join a new company or take on a new role, spend the first few days getting to know your immediate team. There will often be that one person who will reach out and ask you to come along on a tea or lunch break. You should take up that offer. But if no one reaches out, ask if you could join a group. These breaks are a great opportunity to introduce yourself to other people in the team and get to know them. You could also set up individual catch-up meetings with each person in your team, whether you need to work with them or not. Apart from getting to know them, this is also a great way to learn about what is happening in the team. You can start building a working relationship with your colleagues by asking about their work, what they like about their work, or any advice they may have for you. Interacting with your team during your breaks is a way to have conversations beyond work, and you will get to know their likes and dislikes, interests and hobbies. In the beginning, it may be best to avoid personal questions like whether they are married, if they have children, where they studied, where they worked before this, etc. You can find out such details over time. Remember to be open to sharing similar information about yourself as well.

You can also learn a lot about your peers by simply observing them and what is going on around them. You will find out what time they usually get to work, when they are most busy and when they are relatively free in the day, who they usually take breaks with, and so on. Studying their workspace will give you insights into their interests and the people or things that are important to them. To show your interest in getting to know them better, you could bring up something you noticed on their table. Since these are things that they have put out on public display, they are likely to be a lot more open to talking about it.

At times, you might wonder if when trying to connect with members of your team you are wasting their time. While you can try and look at your work in terms of what you can do by yourself, the reality is that most jobs today are highly interdependent. Building relations with people is as much a part of your job as anything else you may do.

Compete with yourself, not your peers

Competition is a part of every aspect of life. Organizations, teams and even individuals are seen to be in constant competition with each other to get ahead and be seen as more valuable. You can change that framework by choosing to compete only with yourself. Ask yourself if you are being the best *you* can be? Are you reaching out for all the opportunities that *you* want?

As you stretch yourself and grow, more work will flow your way. Instead of focusing on competing with your colleagues, focus on becoming better at your job, and let the relevant people in your organization know that you are ready for more responsibility. There will be times when a well-deserved promotion or a desired role doesn't come your way – you will feel disappointed or disheartened. A good way to deal with such disappointment is to ask for feedback on what you could have done better or what you need to do, and be more prepared the next time a similar opportunity arises.

Everyone within an organization is ultimately working to help it grow to the next level or move ahead of the competition. You may also someday find that your organization may not be growing as fast as you would like or that good opportunities for growth just do not exist in that environment. In this case, you should certainly look for a role outside your organization. However, in most cases, there is always an opportunity to grow – and if you grow, you help the organization grow.

The real competition is outside your organization

Sometimes, we get so caught up in proving how right we are, how our team is better than the others, how our ideas are superior, that we forget that the real competition is outside the organization. Everyone within the organization is working together to beat the competition – those within aren't the competition.

> **Off the record**
>
> Pushy colleagues who are always wanting to win often appear to be getting ahead faster than you. In their hurry to get ahead, if they step on too many toes or make too many enemies, it will catch up with them.

Getting ahead in your career is a great goal, but ensure that you do this while getting along with people around you and taking them along with you. Working with peers is all about balancing collaboration and competition. However, this doesn't mean agreeing with everything that others are saying. There will be times when you have a difference of opinion, a disagreement, or will feel let down by a peer. The best way to deal with conflicts is to have a frank and direct conversation with the person you are having trouble with. While very useful, these are sure to be some of the most difficult conversations that you will ever have.

Don't avoid difficult conversations

Here's a scenario that is likely to play out multiple times in your professional life. You may feel angry and let down because a colleague didn't complete their work on time and you eventually had to do all their work as well. The colleague on their part might be wondering why you didn't follow-up or remind them about the work if the deadline was approaching and was critical.

If you decide to discuss the issue with your colleague, prepare to have a difficult conversation. The first obstacle you will face is that both of you may see the same incident differently. You may have assumed that your colleague would complete the work as committed, while your colleague may be thinking that you should've reminded them if it was so important.

The second difficulty is that feelings are always involved in difficult conversations. You may wonder, 'Should I be feeling this way? How does the other person feel about this situation? If I were to bring up the subject and say what I'm feeling, would it make the other person angry or hurt? Would it make matters even worse?' It is usual to worry about whether people will think poorly of us, because we choose to address an issue. The questions that are raised include: Does my having an issue with this situation make me a less competent person? Will my peer see me as less collaborative?

All of these factors make it very difficult and uncomfortable to have conversations that can help resolve conflicts or differences. So what do most people do? They ignore the conflict by downplaying it. Or, they wait for the issue to go away in time, which it sometimes does, but there is no guarantee that it will. Sometimes, people railroad their way through a conflict, ignoring the other person's perspective and feelings altogether. In the short term, it may seem like you have won the argument, but if you force opinions too many times, you are likely to build anger and animosity within your peers. The best way out of such situations is to talk things out with the other person involved. Most issues are resolved this way. Even if things may not have panned out exactly the way you wanted, there will at least be some progress towards dialogue with your colleagues.

Look at this instance where an awkward situation had to be dealt with: Reema (name changed) had joined a consulting firm and was working on a project with a senior colleague who had been in the organization much longer than her. This colleague had a sharp tongue and could be very critical when Reema made the smallest error. Worse, their office was small, and the way she behaved with Reema was on full display. Reema was often sad and demotivated because of this behaviour, and wasn't sure how she was to deal with this situation. On the one hand, Reema's colleague was knowledgeable and Reema needed to work with her. On the other hand, this kind of behaviour was really sapping her energy. Finally, Reema decided to talk to her

> **Off the record**
>
> Most people have strong likes and dislikes, ideas of right and wrong, or good and bad. These are 'unconscious biases'. Getting along requires us to suspend our biases and learn to look at the world from others' point of view.

and share how she felt. Reema explained to her colleague that although she didn't mind being pulled up when she made mistakes, doing this in front of other colleagues felt very disrespectful to her. The colleague didn't stop being critical, but she did stop making her remarks in front of other colleagues. Over time, their relationship improved and as Reema got better at her job, the critical feedback also decreased.

Difficult conversations are just that – difficult. They make both parties uncomfortable as there are emotions involved on either side. The sooner you learn to have such conversations, the easier they become in your professional life.

It will become easier to have difficult conversations in the workplace if you keep these three rules in mind.

1. You are not always right and the other party is not always wrong.
2. Both parties want the same thing, but your approaches to getting there may be different.
3. Both parties want the same thing but believe that only one of you will get it. Try finding solutions in which both of you gain and lose equally.

If you find that you are still having difficulty having these conversations, you could get a copy of the book *Difficult Conversations* by Douglas Stone, Bruce Patton and Sheila Heen, where they provide step-by-step guidelines on how to improve your skills at having difficult conversations.[1] Despite all your efforts, remember that not all issues may be or can be resolved at your level. Nevertheless, you should try to resolve them yourself before resorting to an escalation to your manager.

Dealing with escalations to managers

There will nevertheless be times when you have tried everything possible to resolve an issue with a peer and find that you are still getting nowhere. At such times, you should bring your manager into the conversation. First, present the situation to the manager honestly and objectively without bad-mouthing the other person. This will help your manager remain neutral and balanced. It is also important to let your manager know the details about the conflict and what you have done to resolve it. This will help because your manager can then present your perspective to the other people involved. They may also be able to guide you and suggest alternate courses of action or mentor your colleague. If your conflict is with people in other teams, your manager may then need to engage with the manager of the other team to resolve the issue and help you move forward.

Long-term career success depends on your ability to build effective relationships with your peers. There is another equally, if not even more, important relationship you must maintain well and that is the one with your manager. Managing your manager and building an effective working relationship with your manager is also critical to career success, and this is what we will address in the next chapter.

Tips and Takeaways

- Career success is determined by your ability to get along with others and build strong relationships.
- Relations with your team members are important for getting work done. Relations with people in other team help you develop broader understanding of the business and future career moves.
- Giving and asking for help is the most natural way relationships are built at work. Asking for help doesn't mean you are incompetent.
- Leading and following are both important. This means that sometimes you will let your colleagues lead and you will follow.
- Working with peers is about balancing competition and collaboration. You can get ahead even as you get along with people with whom you work.
- When working with peers, disagreements and conflicts are unavoidable. Talking through the disagreements is the best way forward. These conversations will be some of the most uncomfortable and difficult conversations of your working life, but they must be carried out.

5

MANAGING THE BOSS

Have you ever felt that the success of your career seems to depend as much on your boss liking you as on how well you work? If your answer is yes, you are not alone. A well-known secret of organizational world is that your success depends on your relationship with your boss (and your boss's boss) to a large extent. At the same time, it is easy to forget that your boss is equally dependent on you. For his/her success, your manager is being evaluated not only on his/her own work but also on the quality of work performed by the team. If you don't perform well, your manager suffers as well because the overall performance of the team suffers.

In this chapter, we will discuss the reciprocal dependency between managers and the people who report to them and explore how this relationship can be made more productive and mutually beneficial. If you understand that your manager and you have a mutual need – your need to do well and your manager's need for you to do well – performing well will become far more effortless.

As a young professional, you will value being self-sufficient and will want to prove that you can be trusted to work independently. Your manager *also* wants you to be independent because it will make their life easier. Nevertheless, remember that your manager is your main link to the organization, and can help you prioritize your work and get you the information and resources required to do your job well. Harvard Business School professors John Gabarro and John Kotter write in their much-cited article 'Managing Your Boss'[1] that most people fail to see that their managers can get severely hurt by their actions, and that honesty and cooperation are needed for a work relationship to be effective. At the very minimum, managers expect you to be reliable, to do your job well and keep them informed about any developments while doing your job. Many make the mistake of believing that they are self-sufficient and don't need much help from a boss. They forget that their manager is an important connection to the rest of the organization. Your manager assigns you your work goals and helps align your work with organizational needs.

Some managers are really good at anticipating what their team members need and are good at taking care of their people. However, as Gabarro and Kotter say, bosses are also human and fallible. Not all bosses are good at caring for their people. Those who are effective at work understand this, and don't wait for help to be offered or information to be shared by their manager – they make sure that they get the help and information that they need to do their job. However, 'managing up' is not about brown-nosing or, as we say in India, *chamchagiri*. As Gabarro and Kotter advise, managing up is about understanding your boss well and using that information to build and maintain a healthy working relationship with your boss. If you begin to consider this an important aspect of your job, you will be more open to doing some of the things that we are going to discuss. Managing up begins with attempting to understand your manager – what motivates them, what are their business goals and how can you help them succeed at what they wish to accomplish.

Understanding your manager

Understanding your manager includes not only being sensitive about your manager's professional expectations of you, but also making some allowances for their personality. For example, if you know that your manager is not a morning person, don't schedule early-morning or start-of-the-day meetings that involve her. Give her some time to settle in at her desk and then interact. These are small gestures but they require you to observe and understand your boss. Many people are unable to establish a good equation with their managers to begin with because they haven't taken the time to understand them.

Try and keep abreast of your manager's goals, objectives and critical priorities. Ask for information, pay attention to your boss's behaviours and test assumptions by asking questions. This is an important exercise not just with a new boss but also with someone you have been reporting to for a while because work priorities keep evolving over time. You will find that most managers are reasonably helpful. The best way to get the information you need is to maintain a regular flow of information between you and your manager.

Staying in touch with your manager

One of the first things you should check on is your manager's preferences on how to be reached. Emails are an efficient way to keep your manager updated. Ensure that you also check with your manager about what information she wants to be copied (cc'd) in on. You could forward emails that she is not marked on if you think it is useful information. Thse are quick and easy ways to keep information flowing regularly.

Although cc'ing people on an email is a quick way to keep all stakeholders informed, remember that when a manager is brought into the cc, it is often interpreted as an escalation. When communicating with people at your level, copying your manager on an email could be wrongly interpreted as your trying to get a higher-up's attention. Unless the email deals with a matter that you deliberately wish to escalate, be careful when cc'ing people on emails.

> **Off the record**
>
> You may have a boss who seems to be always testing you, challenging you or saying things like, 'If you are so smart, prove it.' If you sense that your boss is of this type, seek help elsewhere.

If your manager hasn't already set it up, ask for regular one-on-one meetings with her. These meetings could be fairly frequent if you are new to your role, have a new manager or if you are going to work on a very important project. You can adjust the frequency of these meetings later, but the most important thing is to make sure that these meetings take place. Don't cancel, or allow your manager to cancel, a meeting; instead reschedule it. Once you get a meeting on the calendar, there is a higher probability that you will end up meeting. Remember that both your time and your manager's time is precious, so use it well.

Using your time well

Preparing ahead for your meetings with your manager is an efficient way to utilize your time. Make a list of what you want to share or ask your manager in advance. Instead of using your meeting with your manager for a mere status update, which can easily be provided via email, you could use the time to discuss how you should be approaching your work. Brainstorm ideas and ask for suggestions related to your work. You will find that these meetings will also help you better understand your manager – her working style, what's important to her, her way of thinking.

You could consider sharing the contents of your one-on-one meetings with your peers (other people who report to your manager). Their perspectives will help gain a more nuanced understanding of your manager. What's more, sharing this information will also help you build a relationship with your colleagues.

Here are some ideas to start building a healthy and effective relationship with your manager.

Building a healthy working relationship

Know your job – and do it!

The best way to build a healthy relationship with your manager is to know your job and do it well. Sometimes, even your manager may not have clarity about your role. You can work with your manager to define your role more clearly. You can also talk to other people in the organization and observe what is happening in different divisions, reflect on what you are good at and what you wish to do, and, finally, use this information to identify some key result areas (KRAs) for your role.

Have honest conversations

A good habit to build early in your career is to have candid conversations with your manager about what you need from her and what she expects from you. You are better off not assuming what is expected of you. Further, it is better to ask for what you require rather than hope that your manager will guess what you need.

Know yourself

> **Off the record**
>
> Many bosses like 'yes-men' however, in the long run this is not a sustainable success strategy.

Reflect on where you will most need your manager's help to do your work efficiently. Most importantly, know your own reaction to authority. Do you naturally resist authority? Are you likely to become rebellious or resentful when you are asked to do something by your manager? If any of your key needs are not being met, is it likely to show up as discontent in the workplace? For example, for some people, getting public recognition for work well done is an important motivation. If your manager doesn't place much importance on recognizing you or you work, your dissatisfaction may show up in your performance and you must be cautious about this.

Later in the book, we will share more ways for you to reflect and understand yourself better – your personality, key motivators, and under-stress behaviours. Your manager can be a good source of feedback as you learn to adapt your behaviour to meet situational demands.

Learn to anticipate your boss's needs

What problems is your manager trying to solve for the organization? How can you help her do her job better? Pay attention and be genuinely helpful to the boss. For example, if your manager has a review meeting every Wednesday, make sure she has all the information she needs.

During the course of your job, problems will always arise. By bringing them up at the right time in the right manner, you can get the attention that you need and a resolution that works for you.

Expressing disagreements with the boss

When is it alright to disagree with your boss? A smart trick to figure out is not only *when*, but also *how* to disagree with a boss. If you have ideas that you think will give better results, even if they may be different from what your boss wants you to do, speak up. Do this privately, at a time when you know your boss is likely to be more receptive to your ideas. Be clear and specific when saying why you disagree and what you would like to do instead. If your boss still disagrees, commit to their way of doing things and do it well.

Mentors, stakeholders and sponsors

Although we have primarily discussed handling your relationship with your manager, managing up is also about finding mentors and sponsors within the organization. Mentors are experienced professionals in the organization who can help you understand your work and provide insights based on their experience. You may want to start looking around early to identify potential mentors. Try to choose mentors who are at least at your manager's level or at higher levels of the organization. This helps you see the big picture of the organization.

It is also a good idea to build congenial working relations with your manager's peers and other stakeholders who are important to your team's success. These congenial relations will help your manager become more effective in her role and generally build goodwill for you, your manager and your team.

Sponsors are people who are willing to openly support the advancement of your career. Gaining sponsorship requires you to identify people who will be important to the growth of your career, usually people beyond your manager. Taking initiative to get on projects that will bring you that visibility and doing well on those projects is a good way to build such relationships. Like your manager, mentors, stakeholders and sponsors also want you to be collaborative, reliable and honest.

Off the record

You will encounter managers who are disinterested (in you), over-worked or incompetent. Your best bet in these situations is to remain focused on doing your work, finding mentors who can help you, and showing patience and confidence.

Dealing with a difficult manager

There will be times in your career where you will have a difficult manager and working with them might end up being really stressful. Always remember that your manager is also a human being and has human failings. As you get to know your manager better, you will begin to notice some of their blind spots, their weaknesses that they may be unaware of. Step back and reflect on whether your own behaviour is contributing in any way to the tension in your relationship. At the beginning of this chapter, we had said that a manager expects you to be reliable, cooperative and honest. Are you fulfilling these responsibilities?

Sometimes, you may find that your manager is genuinely struggling in her role for a variety of reasons. You still need to remain focused on your needs, which are to seek clarity, information and resources to do your job well. In this scenario, knowing your job and doing it well becomes even more relevant because you may need to step up and take charge of your career. If you are not getting the information or resources that you need to do your job well, it may require you to talk to others in the organization or reach out to your manager's manager for help.

> **Off the record**
>
> You will learn from 'good' managers and you will learn from 'bad' managers. Bad managers will teach you what not to do when you become a manager. The experience will also teach you how to fend for yourself.

Practice genuine compassion and acknowledge that your manager is not perfect. To the greatest extent that you can, try and help bolster a manager's weaker areas. For example, if you have noticed that your manager doesn't enjoy detailed spreadsheets and data analysis, and this is an area that you are good at or don't mind stretching yourself in, volunteer to help out. Of course, there are times when you may find that you are temperamentally incapable of working with your manager or that they do not inspire you in any way. Typically, this is far less common than you think. In case you have tried everything and you are still stuck, you may ask to be assigned another manager. It is important to not let your career be derailed because of a boss you can't work with. Navigate past these career blocks and, no matter what you do, don't bad-mouth your manager. This is a situation in which mentors and sponsors can be very helpful.

Finally, successfully managing up is not about sycophancy, *chamchagiri* or merely pleasing higher-ups. It is about making an active effort to understand your manager and building a healthy and positive relationship with senior colleagues. Good relations with your higher-ups are a source of power and can come with a certain influence. And as a young professional, it is usually best to build your bases of power as soon as you can.

Tips and Takeaways

- Your career success often depends on your relationship with your boss; and whether they understand it or not, your boss is equally dependent on you for their success.
- Managing up is not sycophancy. It is about building an effective working partnership with your boss.
- Highly effective people make sure they get the information and help they need from their manager. They don't wait for it to be provided.
- Staying in touch with your manager and keeping a regular flow of information to your manager is always a good idea. Consider it a part of your job.

- There are times when you may find that you are just temperamentally incapable of working with your manager. Find a way around this. You cannot allow your career to be derailed because of a poor fit with a manager.
- Do not bad-mouth your manager. Learn to be effective and noticed by other people instead.

6

POWER AND POLITICS

Few words are treated with as much ambivalence in an organization as 'power' and 'politics'.

As young professionals starting out in our careers, we were determined to never play a 'political' game or abuse our 'power' (if and when we had any). While we did manage to live by these intentions through most of our careers, it also became clear that without at least understanding these realities that exist in all organizations, one would find it difficult to achieve success in them.

Honestly, there is no organization where power and politics are not important realities. This applies even to organizations where you would least expect this to be the case, such as in volunteer-based organizations, academic organizations, spiritual organizations or any other institution where people come together for altruistic reasons and not for private gain. But ironically, sometimes the most bitter political battles are played out in just these organizations. As a result, understanding the nuances of how power and politics work is central to your ability to do well in your organizational career. At the start of your career, this understanding will help you stay out of trouble. Later, as you gain more experience, it will help you successfully navigate an organization. Right at the top of the organization, it could be key to your ability to get anything done.

In this chapter, we will help you develop a better idea of how power and politics function in the workplace. We will also show you how you can navigate tricky situations where these forces are at play in the early years of your career.

My first brush with politics: Caught in the crossfire

Many years ago, I (Shalini) naïvely walked into the crossfire of a political battle without realizing it.

Early in my career, I had joined an industrial tools company to manage training and development. One of my key responsibilities was managing the management trainee programme for the organization. My boss at the time was almost four decades older than me, and to me seemed completely uninterested in any new ideas at all. Back then, you needed to write out ideas and suggestions in internal memos that would be filed, and then take these files physically to your boss and leave them at their desk. Well, all my ideas seemed to go into his room to die. I never heard back on anything and whenever I asked, he responded with great sarcasm.

Not surprisingly, my relationship with my boss was rather strained. Sometimes, days went by without us speaking and when we did meet, our meetings would be very stressful. Everyone across the organization seemed to feel the same way about him, yet this didn't seem to affect his position at the company. In contrast, all young people in the organization looked up to another senior leader – the head of International Business. Let's call him Jim. Jim was a dashing, handsome, very bright high-flyer who was known to be close to the managing director, and rumoured to be next in line to take over the reins of the company.

One day, Jim called me in to discuss the high rate of attrition for management trainees in the international business division. He spoke about how the company just didn't seem to understand what the trainees' aspirations were and he wanted to do a survey to understand why they had left. I thought this was a great idea, but given my past experiences, I didn't discuss this survey with my boss. I was sure it would lead to him simply sitting on the suggestion, or worse, a dose of his trademark bitter sarcasm. So I went along with Jim's suggestions, and we designed an employee engagement survey for all management trainees. In fact, I justified my omission by telling myself that since I was administering the management trainee programme, it was up to me to decide how to make it better. And collecting feedback was definitely a step in the right direction. Perhaps, my boss would eventually come around and tell me that I had done a good job.

Through all of this preparation and excitement, what I had failed to recognize was that there was something very wrong about how this was playing out. I eased my nervousness by telling myself that even though my boss was not in the know, I still had Jim from senior management in on this, and it was all the same. Through all this, I saw Jim as a visionary. It didn't strike me that Jim stepping into territory that was not his (the HR function in this case) would ruffle feathers, bruise egos and potentially lead to serious miscommunication within the company.

A few days later, a questionnaire with a cover note from Jim went out to every management trainee. As the questionnaire went out, I was delighted to think that I was part of making this positive change. However, the reality of what I had done began to sink in once I started getting calls from people asking why Jim's signature was on the mail instead of my boss's. Soon, it seemed everyone in my company knew about this. There were whispers within the organization that Jim and my boss had an argument regarding this in a senior team meeting. A week later, my boss, the HR Head, called me to his room, and he had not been happy.

I have thought about this incident often over the years, and I'm still amazed at how little I understood politics and organizations at the time. With the benefit of experience and age, it is now obvious that in my admiration for Jim and my discomfort with my own boss, I had failed to see the political game being played between him and Jim. And I had willingly played along as a pawn. I can now think of far better ways to have dealt with the situation, but I was truly naïve (and perhaps a little stupid) when it came to understanding political strategies and sensitivities.

No matter how I felt about my own boss, it was wrong of me to not have informed him about what we were doing. Despite the fact that Jim had so confidently asked me to draft and send out the survey, I should have realized that by keeping the HR head out of the conversation, he was playing a very dangerous game of one-upmanship. It is my hope that you will be far smarter and be able to recognize when a political game is afoot and have the good sense to stay out of it.

Power

The textbook definition of power is 'the ability to get things done' in a specific way. On the face of it, this is a perfectly innocent definition. After all, organizations are all about getting things done, so why should there be any discomfort with games of power? The fact of the matter is, power is one of the most sought-after commodities in an organization.

Sometimes, power is sought as a means to an end. For instance, having power will help you do more for the organization. It allows you to have a greater say in important decisions or to get others to follow your ideas and suggestions. In organizations, having power is often closely connected with having status and it is often sought after for this reason too. For instance, when you have power, you will be consulted more, things are likely to go your way more often. Of course, there are the perks of power: greater organizational status, a good job title, a better salary, a better office. All of these are markers of success in our society. So, it stands to reason that power is a very valued commodity in most organizations.

But then why are so many people uncomfortable with the idea of power and politics?

Off the record

There are lots of people who have reached the top without waging political wars. But they usually do understand the political landscape enough to not make too many political mistakes.

Discomfort with power

Perhaps one of the big fears we have about power play is that someone in authority will make us do things we do not want to do. This is not an entirely unreasonable fear because people do misuse their power to get subordinates to do unethical deeds. This could range from sexual harassment to falsifying information to very serious transgressions of integrity. The allegations in the 2018 #MeToo movement are an example of what happens when power is misused. The entire financial meltdown in 2008 also had people in positions of power misusing their power to do unethical things that in the short term had made them look good.

In the course of your career, someone powerful may one day ask you to falsify information, pay a bribe to someone else or share privileged information with someone who perhaps should not have access to it. It is important that you remember that only you will ultimately be held accountable for your actions, irrespective of who asked you to do what. 'Following orders' never cuts it as a justification. Your choices will boil down to how strong your own internal moral compass is and how much courage you have in that moment. Our character is revealed through moments like these, and the decision you take (or don't take) is yours alone.

Off the record

- Become a careful observer of how decisions are being taken in your organization. You can learn a lot about the political landscape.
- Build multiple bases of power. Designations are only one among many displays of power.
- Treat your reputation with care. It is one of your most valuable assets.

While you may never encounter such dilemmas, these kinds of transgressions or incidents of misuse of power occur fairly frequently. They are real events with very unfortunate consequences for everyone involved. If you ever find yourself in such a situation, please reach out at once to your HR department or an approachable senior leader. If you observe someone being bullied by a person in power, reach out to the person being bullied, assure them of your support and help them think through all the ways in which they can act.

But sometimes, discomfort with power isn't about an ethical clash. Your discomfort may stem from something else. It may be the fact that the person in power may have a working style very different from your own, and you may feel uncomfortable about having to do things in a way that is completely different from what you are accustomed to. This dance of power is the reality of every organization and as we will discuss later, you simply *will* have to find your way to work with this.

Discomfort with politics

Being uncomfortable with politics is even more common than feeling discomfort with power. There are some good reasons why you may find politics in a workplace, and indeed in human interactions, distasteful. You may have seen colleagues play politics in the office, and thoughtlessly betray the confidence of their colleagues. Sometimes, they may actively work against what is good for others in their teams only because it serves their own interests. You may also find it very upsetting when what you feel are inferior solutions win over far better solutions only because the person suggesting them has influence in the office.

In my experience, no one really likes highly political workplaces, even those who are extremely adept at handling political games. This is because there is something deeply unsettling about organizations where influence routinely belongs to those who are seen as less competent. The human need for justice is far stronger than you may expect. In fact, it is not just humans – even other primates feel upset when they view an outcome that does not seem fair.

Primates and Justice

A study conducted at Emory University in Atlanta suggested that our sense of justice seems to be hardwired in us through evolution.[1] It may have evolved from a need to live fairly in large and complex groups, in the same way as primates still do.

Brosnan and her colleague Frans de Waal taught brown capuchin monkeys (*Cebus apella*) to swap plastic tokens for food. Normally, monkeys were happy to exchange a token for some cucumber. But the monkeys took offence if they saw a neighbour getting a grape for a token. In about half of such trials, the short-changed capuchin either refused to hand over its token or rejected the reward. Some threw the token or cucumber clean out of their cage. The animals' umbrage was even greater if another monkey got a grape for nothing. About 80 per cent rebelled in some way in this situation.

The reality of organizational life is that power and politics are so tightly intertwined with the daily work done in an office that it is nearly impossible to disentangle rewards and influence in any simple way. This is a very, very important lesson for anyone who is part of the organizational world. You need to understand how power and politics work to be effective in this world and it is our hope that you will not abuse this understanding for personal gain.

Coming to terms with power

Fundamental maturing, or growing up, occurs when you come to terms with the reality of power in organizations. It is a truth that cannot be denied: some people simply have more power than others. And those who have more power are able to have greater influence on organizational outcomes than those who do not. They are invited to the most important meetings, their views are heard with greater attention and it is far easier for them to find allies for their ideas. Those without power, on the other hand, tend to find themselves struggling to be heard.

So how does one become more 'power'ful in an organization? It turns out that power is not simply dependent on the seniority of the role you are in, though that is often part of it. There are in fact many other ways to gain power. In 1959, social psychologists John R. P. French and Bertram Raven listed five important bases or sources of power.

This model (depicted on the following page) is still one of the most influential in understanding the many ways in which power grows.

The two sources of power that are perhaps the easiest to understand are reward power and coercive power. As the name suggests, *reward power* is the power of an individual to give rewards to others for doing what is expected from them. These rewards could be of many kinds. They could be in the familiar promotions or performance pay or they could be less tangible rewards such as visibility, recognition or a positive

Sources of Power

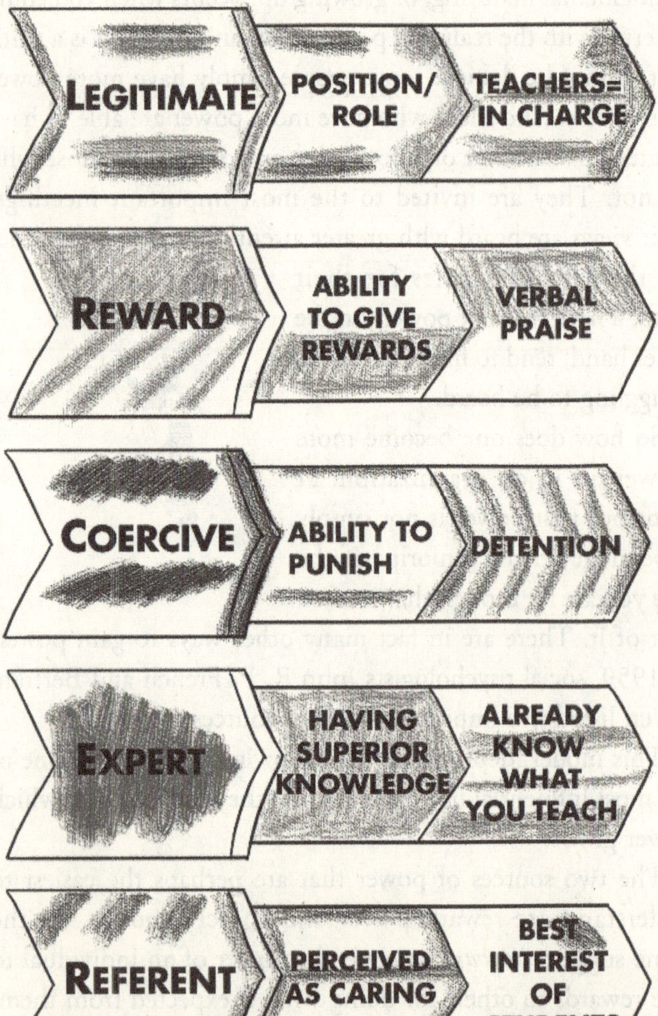

recommendation to a critical senior. *Coercive power* is the ability to punish someone for not doing something that is expected of them. This could take the form of denying any desired rewards such as promotions and pay hikes, bad-mouthing you or even firing you. Unsurprisingly, both these bases of power are highly situational. The moment the situation changes, they lose their power.

The other three bases of power need a bit of explanation.

Legitimate power is power that is based on company hierarchy or roles. We listen to our bosses (for the most part!) because it is their role to give us direction. Most of us, under most circumstances, want to play by the rules, and so we allow people in positions of legitimate power to guide our actions. This could include a variety of people from managers at work to the cabin crew on a flight to the traffic constable on the road when he pulls you over.

Expert power comes from being seen as an authority in a particular sphere. This is power gained from being a qualified professional, such as a doctor, lawyer or professor, or a well-known writer or thought leader within a particular field. We tend to listen to expert opinions because we believe that they have expertise and hence authority in a certain field.

Referent power comes from being the influencers in a group. This is demonstrated when you start believing in something because someone you admire in your group of peers believes in it. Another way in which referent power plays out is when our thought process is influenced by those we admire. Social media influencers often rely on referent power as people listen to them because they admire them.

Building your power through social networks

Have you ever thought of building your power by developing and expanding your social and professional networks?

We have found that this is an idea that frequently divides people. Some people take a very matter-of-fact approach to networking. After hearing the importance of networking being repeated at many business forums, they accept that networking is an important skill and activity and simply get on with it. As a result, they may reach out to people at conferences or public events, exchange cards and with seeming effortlessness set up and develop their networks.

> **Think about it!**
>
> - What are your primary sources of power?
> - What sources of power can you build on?
> - What are the implications of your power bases?

For many others, this is a very difficult idea to come to terms with. These people usually feel deeply uncomfortable with the idea of meeting people and building relationships based on their 'utility'. They may even look at efficient networkers and see them as insincere and political individuals. And yet, at the same time, they may know that by not having effective networks, they are missing out on many opportunities. So what can one do?

However you feel about networking, there is ample research that points to one thing. Having good networks at work is key to being effective both in a particular role and throughout your career. I repeat, having good networks is key to being effective in the immediate and in the long term.

You can definitely do your job well on the strength of sheer hard work and brilliance. But there are many jobs and roles that simply cannot be done without a strong network. For instance, imagine a job that requires the support of many people in your organization, particularly of people who are not part of your team and who do not follow the same systems as your division – let's say you are an HR business partner or a sales manager or work process engineer. You will need to work with many people who do not report to you or even to a common senior manager. It is not always possible for your manager to create these bridges for you. You will need to learn to navigate these relationships yourself and to do this, you will need networks.

> **Off the record**
>
> Effective networking is an art form of its own. The best networkers are constantly building bridges for everyone else – not burning them.

The importance of strong networks only increases as you rise up the ranks of an organization. To the inexperienced eye, it may appear that all you need to do to rise in the ranks is to put your head down and work and then you will be effective. But the fact is, the more senior you are, the more your job will rely on others outside your formal authority. For instance, although an HR head has control over only a small team, they need to have the entire organization complete their performance appraisals by a certain date to mark that project as complete. A marketing head needs to work with sales, strategy and PR teams internally and many media outlets and influencers externally to be effective. You will be responsible for work that requires the input of many others, with only a few of whom may report directly to you.

To complete all such tasks you need good networks.

What do we know about building networks other than the fact that they are key to our ability to be effective?

First, we know that effective networks are built over time. Like any relationship, professional networks take time and care to develop. This is perhaps unsurprising. After all, relationships develop or unfold through trusting each other and trust takes time to build. So, while exchanging visiting cards is often a good starting point, you must realize that it is just that. Knowing someone's name is very different from building a relationship of trust and reciprocity. And it is this trust and reciprocity that will be important to making relationships that last.

Second, we know that relationships thrive on reciprocity. What this means is that generosity begets generosity and pettiness begets pettiness. How can you use the principle of reciprocity? Be generous and giving in your relationships with others to start with. Many will respond to such thoughtfulness with similar reciprocity, and over time, your relationship will deepen.

Networking experts emphasize not to be seen as being a taker in a relationship. Learn to be a giver while developing your network. Early on in your career, it may be hard to imagine that many of the relationships you are building are being built for the long term, but that's exactly what you are doing. Being an open and generous professional can only help you because people never really forget petty behaviour.

Third, build your social network *before* you need it. Wouldn't you be far more likely to help someone you have known for a while rather than someone who approaches you only when they need help? Well, the same is true of other people as well. They are more likely to want to work with you if they know you don't just call them when you are asking for a favour. Bonus tip – if you start by building your network early on in your career, as you become more senior, your network will too.

Fourth, learn to say no nicely. You will not always be able to offer and provide help to others. When people are disappointed by not being able to receive help they wanted, they *will* talk about it. When you say no, do so in as nice and sensitive a way as you can. If you can't help, try and offer an alternative solution if possible. These are important career-building skills and will stand you in good stead throughout your career.

Fifth, be consistently professional. Expert networkers believe you can get by with fewer interactions if you are consistently able to be helpful and professional. If you are going to only have a few interactions to build a relationship of trust, make the most of these by being reliable, professional and helpful.

Building your network: Levels of expertise by Prof. Cade Massey[2]

You can learn how to build your network at any level of proficiency. Prof. Cade Massey of Wharton School explains how in his online course on influence.

Level 1: Beginner

A beginner will, at the least, make use of the networking opportunities that are presented to them. These could include being in cross-functional teams, committees, projects, training programmes, etc. Each of these experiences are opportunities to build your network. Say yes to as many such opportunities as you can manage.

Level 2: Intermediate

A person at the intermediate level will create the opportunities that allow them to meet other people. This could mean hosting dinner parties or other networking events and can be very rewarding. As you take the lead in helping others meet and get to know each other, you in turn become connected more deeply to the network, and in a sense act as its anchor. This takes energy, thoughtfulness and effort.

Level 3: Advanced

Not only do people at the advanced level recognize opportunities for networking and create ones that they can, they also consciously expose themselves to situations where networking opportunities may arise. They allow serendipity and chance to play a role, but they go out of their way to be present at opportunities to get to know new people. They understand that sometimes some connections will work out and at other times they won't, but they usually show up at places where there is a possibility of meeting new and different people.

Networks with similar people versus diverse networks

One question that you will have to grapple with sooner or later is whether your network should have similar people or many different kinds of people. Most people find it easier to build and maintain a network of people with similar interests. After all, you are likely to have a common language, a common set of friends and perhaps even a common world view.

However, in 1973, a path-breaking and counter-intuitive paper called 'The Strength of Weak Ties' was published by American sociologist Mark Granovetter.[3] In it, he posits that most of our career opportunities come from our weak ties or from people we don't know that well. This was an interesting idea and got a number of experts wondering: can our weak ties actually be very important?

'The Strength of Weak Ties' is viewed as one of the most influential papers on the operation of social networks. Granovetter surveyed a number of people who had found jobs through their contacts to explore how often they actually met the person who helped them find their current role. Well, it turned out that 56 per cent of the respondents saw their contacts only occasionally, while 28 per cent saw them rarely. This meant that 84 per cent of the ties, or connections, that led to job opportunities were actually 'weak' ties. These weak ties acted as bridges that connected otherwise disconnected social groups. For diffusion of information, it is, therefore, the weak ties that are the most important. And this advice turns out to be very important as you are growing in your career. For example, if you only know people from within your industry, it is likely that you will be approached only for jobs within your industry. On the other hand, if you know people from many different industries, you may learn about opportunities that others will not. So while the idea of weak ties may seem counter-intuitive, it actually makes a lot of sense. As a bonus, being part of several diverse networks will keep you very well informed since you will have access to information from many different circles. This is great for building a broad world view. Think of a diverse network as social capital. It takes a bit of effort to develop and grow but is every bit as useful.

We have one last thought about building networks. Early in your career, you may feel that you will benefit most by reaching out to people in power. However, this is not always easy. Powerful people are usually much sought after and may be less enthusiastic about developing a reciprocal relationship. Networks grow over time, and you may find that people who are at entry-level roles right now may be in positions of power a decade later. It is therefore essential to have some patience and do the right thing by people.

Situation awareness

Now that you understand the concepts of power and politics in an organization, how will you recognize when these play out in your workplace? Well, an essential skill for developing an astute political sense is a sharp sense of situation awareness. Originating from the US military, the term situation awareness refers to the 'perception of elements in the environment, in the volume of time and space, the comprehension of their meaning, and the projection of their status in the near future' (Endsley, 1995).[4] Despite being a rather wordy and academic definition, it is a very useful one.

Situation awareness in organizations means recognizing how power and politics are moving within your organization at any given time. This could mean identifying who is becoming more influential and who is losing influence. It means carefully observing the interactions in your organizations. It also means understanding how alliances are being built in your organization and recognizing the implications of these alliances.

Often, change in organizations takes place gradually. But sometimes, triggered by external shocks or leadership changes, you may find the power dynamics in your organization shift overnight. When you sense your organization is going through such a phase, it is even more important to be situationally aware. You must watch out for and track changes as they unfold across different parts of the organization. You should also try to identify the implications of these changes across the organization and on your work.

> **Off the record**
>
> - The more diverse your network is, the more likely you are to learn of new opportunities, and get new ideas.
> - Always remember that we are genetically wired to feel safe in environments that are perceived as fair. Do your best to create these over time.

Without understanding this landscape of power and politics, performing successfully becomes harder. As you become more senior, whenever you want to advance any organizational agenda, it will require working with the invisible landscape of individual agendas and interests in your organization. You will need to understand and work within this landscape to actually accomplish work.

In conclusion

Power and politics are two of the trickiest areas of organizational life and cause many people much stress. You may see organizational decisions being taken solely to benefit a single individual even if it is to the absolute detriment of the company. And you may see people with poor ideas behave unethically, claiming credit for ideas that weren't theirs, saying one thing to one set of colleagues and another to some others. These behaviours are not only discouraging, they are also demotivating.

There are other far better ways to gain power and influence in organizations. Understanding the different sources of power allows you to have an impact that goes beyond your position in the organization. Building a strong internal (and external) network ensures that you have a good understanding of organizational events and in turn are able to influence these. Now each of these does take a bit of time and effort to develop but then, so do careers. What's more, you will develop a reputation of being well informed, helpful and effective. And that's a winning combination that will take you all the way to the top.

Tips and Takeaways

- Build a wide network. Remember that networks are an important source of power.
- Be the first to give, and generate reciprocity. Generosity is key to building networks.
- Get to know the people in your network and build genuine relationships with them. In the long term, genuineness wins every single time.
- Understand the different interests of different people. Different people are motivated by different factors. Knowledge of this will help you be more effective.
- Not all interests are spoken about or articulated. Try and understand both the spoken and unspoken ones. This will mean moving towards a deeper, nuanced understanding of what people are really seeking.
- Develop support for an idea that is really important to you before the critical decision is to be taken. Often, the best moments to influence someone are in private conversations, away from the public gaze. So, if there is an outcome that

is important to you, try and build acceptance and support for that outcome in your team before it comes to vote.

- Understand that others may be making similar calculations.
- Be cautious about using formal authority in a heavy-handed way. This inevitably builds resentment. Being considerate and gentle will help you use your power effectively without creating resentment.

• •

7

MEN AND WOMEN AT WORK

Each year when the tenth and twelfth standard board and competitive exam results are announced across the country, you'll see a few headlines over and over again in the newspapers that go something like this.

> 'Girls outperform boys! Girl tops scores with 99.5%'
> 'More girls on the IIT JEE's merit list than ever before!'

Given that so many girls come from homes where they are not the preferred child, this is no small accomplishment. After all, they have often overcome indifferent parents and teachers, fewer opportunities to study and far less support for their personal ambitions.

So how does this same intelligence, hard work and resilience play out in the organizational world? Do we see similar stories of success and accomplishment? Can we commonly see women leading the way in corporate India? Sadly, the answer is *no*. This plays out in a few different ways. In some organizations, there are simply too few women employees across the board. This is particularly true of many manufacturing industries. In a lot of organizations, and particularly those in the services industry, there are many women at the entry levels, but diversity thins out considerably as you reach senior management.

There are, however, many wonderful exceptions to the general under-representation of women in industries across the world. The incredibly talented and hardworking women CEOs of Fortune 500 companies include Mary Teresa Barra (General Motors), Virginia Marie 'Ginni' Rometty (IBM), Meg Whitman (Hewlett-Packard), Indra Nooyi (PepsiCo), and Safra Catz (Oracle). Closer home, we have had the examples of Vinita Bali (Britannia Industries), Vinita D. Gupta (Lupin Industries), Aruna Jayanthi (Capgemini), among others.

Women leaders have performed very well as leaders of major business organizations and yet, as of 2017, just 6 per cent of Fortune 500 companies were led by women. And this number has not changed much over several decades. Obviously, there are obstacles in corporate workplaces across the world that make it harder for women to reach the very top. The gender pay gap is real. The Global Wage Report 2018 published by the International Labour Organization[1] put the gender pay gap in India for hourly wages at 34 per cent – among the highest in the world. And in case you are wondering about corporate India, women in top management posts are shown to earn 18.8 per cent less than men, according to a 2016 report by the advisory firm Korn Ferry Hay Group.[2] If women and men are equally talented, then this very stark statistic suggests the presence of several, often invisible, challenges to true meritocracy. However, conversations around how gender affects progress in the workplace are still relatively new.

Sheryl Sandberg's bestselling book, *Lean In*,[3] was truly a breakthrough moment for conversations around gender in the workplace. She spoke about the many reasons why women were under-represented at senior levels and what both men and women could do to change that. After all, if someone as successful, smart and fortunate as her had found it hard to succeed, it stood to reason that regular women find it hard too. A growing field of gender research at global universities presents data that is hard to argue with, and the refreshing emphasis on diversity and inclusion has now allowed us to understand and talk about issues that in the past were simply not on the table. Terms like 'unconscious bias' (bias that operates without a person's awareness), even if poorly understood, are now often part of the conversation at most workplaces in India.

One point that cannot be overemphasized is that *both* men and women make it harder for women in the workplace. They don't mean to, but that is how it plays out. After all, women are no less susceptible to these same unconscious biases. They grow up learning and internalizing the same gender expectations as men from the society they grew up in.

Why is gender parity still a challenge?

Perhaps you are wondering how this can still be an issue. After all, aren't girls and boys receiving similar education, and aren't we seeing both men and women being recruited from college campuses? Though much has changed in the past few decades and women have climbed to the highest echelons of large organizations, you will still see far fewer women than there should be at the very senior levels of business. Here are at least four reasons why.

1. Women are often working two jobs (one in office and one at home) and overtime – that is just exhausting.
2. Women often do prioritize either family or personal well-being over rising up the corporate ladder, and these choices have implications for their careers.
3. There are unconscious biases that lead to both men and women undervaluing women. This makes it harder for women to rise to the top and it often creates an unsatisfying experience at work.
4. Gender stereotypes are still quite alive and make it challenging for women to develop a professional style that is seen as likeable and impactful.

All of these reasons also result in a phenomenon known as the 'leaky bucket of female talent', which alludes to how women keep leaving the corporate world over time.

The first of these reasons – additional societal expectations and responsibilities – is relatively easy to understand. For years, women have been limited by the weight of the expectations surrounding them at all times. We may have seen our mothers, aunts or other women in our circles manage life as working women by getting up early in the morning, getting the family ready for the day and rushing to work. We have then watched them come home in the evening to cook dinner, do a bit more housework, make sure the kids have done their homework, before collapsing in bed at the end of the day. And this cycle begins again the very next day. Across the world, data shows that even today women do the lion's share of the work at home.

The additional work that women do expands manifold when they have children. There are tests to be prepared for, school projects to be finished, extracurricular activities to be participated in, all of which need attention. The responsibility for all of this in many homes still falls to the woman. Over the years, it all becomes simply too exhausting for many women and they begin to question their choices. While not enough is changing fast enough, we can see that some social norms have begun to shift as more women seek a more equal work distribution. Many progressive organizations today have a variety of work policies intended to ease some of the challenges of managing work with family.

Policies that allow women to dial down for a period of time either through work-from-home arrangements or flexi-time are not uncommon now. The extended maternity benefits instituted in India in 2017 are a step in the right direction. All of these measures are very helpful, at least for the few years immediately after childbirth. The challenges of managing both family and work continue for at least a decade more. And eventually, many women choose to dial down the time spent at work or change professions. Despite how daunting these hurdles are, many women do find solutions that work for them. They enlist the help and support of their families, hire help or find schools with after-school activities. But these are not the only concerns for women in the workplace. There are, in fact, many more hurdles.

There is the challenge of ensuring that work environments are safe for all and that sexual harassment is severely dealt with. This is more daunting in some parts of the country, than in others. Even the daily commute by public transport in some parts of the country can make women feel unsafe and create anxiety.

Then there is the challenge of unconscious biases which lead to women being at a disadvantage while being considered for roles or while being evaluated for their competence. Following which, there is the challenge of navigating gender stereotypes not only in the workplace but also within the community. We will discuss many of these in this chapter. But first let's look at what you should know to stay safe.

Dealing with sexual harassment

Sexual harassment works in many different ways to make women (and men) uncomfortable. Sexual harassment as defined by the law includes unwelcome gestures, speech and actions that are sexually colourful and inappropriate in the workplace. These acts create a disturbing and stressful environment for the victim, but fortunately there are a growing number of workplaces committed to creating a safe environment. Sexual harassment can also operate in a much more subtle but equally disturbing fashion. Here it operates as pressure to give time and attention to a powerful person or else face the consequences. This is far trickier to deal with as it is very difficult to prove, or sometimes, even to realize what is going on. No lewd comments are exchanged and no gesture overtly occurs. Yet it operates and influences workplace decisions.

The #MeToo movement has been a long time coming and for the first time it has taken away the impunity associated with obvious acts of harassment. This is a very big shift in conversation and will, one hopes, shift the power dynamic between men and women in the workplace too. For the very first time, we have seen women come together to name and shame heinous offenders, many of who have escaped scrutiny for decades.

There have also been some very big shifts in the legal framework surrounding sexual harassment. A landmark Supreme Court judgment in 2013 now mandates that all organizations with more than 10 employees need to have an Internal Complaints Committee to investigate charges of sexual harassment.

What to do if you are being sexually harassed in the workplace?

A senior advisor in a Big Four (Deloitte, EY, KPMG and PwC) consulting firm says that one of the main reasons that sexual harassment in the workplace doesn't get reported as often as it should is because victims don't recognize that they have legal rights. They are also often discouraged because they are not sure if what happened to them is to be classified as harassment. The first step then is to understand what constitutes sexual harassment under the law.

There are a range of activities, gestures and postures that are defined under the Sexual Harassment of Women at Workplace (Prevention, Prohibition, and Redressal) Act of 2013, making it clear as to what qualifies as sexual harassment. The act has a wide, universal scope, and it applies to full-time and part-time employees, probationers and apprentices, contract and daily wage labourers. Apart from being applicable to all sorts of organizations and entities, the law also applies to places that an employee needs to visit for official purposes, including transportation provided by the employer.

Once the incident(s) has been identified as a case of sexual harassment, one could either try to address the issue personally or directly file a complaint. You can address this directly if you feel safe and empowered in the context. Most cases of sexual harassment however can't be addressed personally, leaving the victim with no option but to file a complaint. Before filing a complaint, it is important to understand the company's policies as well as the law of the country in detail. It is helpful to record the incident(s) in any relevant form. These may take the form of any emails, texts, etc. that were exchanged. Sometimes CCTV footage may also be relevant.

Having been through an extremely emotionally disturbing time, it is difficult for anyone to approach a course of action objectively. However, objectivity and calm in formulating a complaint helps the complainant succeed. Dealing with investigations may also feel equally challenging. The complainant must be patient to ensure that the incident is viewed fairly. Sometimes the complainant may have a specific punishment in mind for the aggressor and seek it during the investigative process. However, one must count on the law to direct the course of justice.

Finally, remember that recovering from an incident of sexual harassment can take time. It will require accepting the incident and knowing that you have taken recourse under the available law. Your safety is supremely important. And you must do whatever you can to stay safe always. And with that important consideration, let's take a closer look at other reasons why women face additional hurdles as they build their careers.

The role of biology and society

Perhaps the most obvious of reasons why women are underrepresented in organizations is also one of the easiest to understand: the role of biology and of society.

Women can have babies and men can't. And when human babies are born, they need to be taken care of – a role that has traditionally been expected of women. Over the course of human evolution, it is women who have often stayed at home to look after babies while men have gone out and searched for food. Over tens of thousands of years, in almost all societies around the world, women became the primary (or even the sole) caregivers, while men went out to earn a living. As a result, women became associated with the task of nurturing and looking after the children and family while men got associated with the task of going out and earning the bread.

Now compared to the long history of humankind, women have entered the organization very recently. Your mother, or even you, might be the first generation of working women in your family. What this means is that sometimes without even being aware of it, we have different expectations from ourselves or from women in our workplaces than we do from men. As a result, many working mothers have to deal with the phenomenon of 'mommy guilt', a feeling of neglecting or letting down their kids in some way because they are away working. This is a near universal phenomenon across all cultures and can create tremendous stress for young mothers.

This stress itself makes working with little kids a very different experience for women and men. We are encouraged by the fact that in recent years there is a growing recognition of the importance of more family-friendly policies that will make it easier for women (and men) to manage being parents while being at work.

Although conversations surrounding gender stereotyping are finally happening, there are other challenges that are not immediately obvious when you enter the workplace, as is discussed below.

Conscious or unconscious bias at work

Bias can operate at two levels. The first, is the kind that manifests itself as a bias against women in certain roles and can come from a belief that women are not well suited to a particular role. And these biases may be held by anyone in the organization – your senior, your peers, or even external partners you work with.

Several years ago, I (Shalini) had joined, for a leadership-level role, an organization where there were almost no women at any level. My entry into the organization as a senior leader was perhaps a bit unusual for the organization. A few weeks after I had joined, a young man in a one-on-one meeting confessed that he was not comfortable working with a woman leader. He shared that he had worked with women before, and on the whole, he thought they were difficult and insecure as colleagues. A part of me was rather relieved that he had shared his discomfort openly instead of quietly letting it impact his work on the team. However, another part was saddened by how much harder my job was going to be. After all, if he had said what was on his mind, there were sure to be many others who felt similarly but simply hadn't voiced it.

This was a challenge that my male colleagues would never have to face. Similarly, there are organizations that would not pick women for certain roles – a decision they make quite consciously. For instance, there are companies that will never pick women for roles that require interactions with unions or for roles that require extensive travel or irregular hours.

In these situations, there is clearly a clash between the beliefs that our society holds about the 'appropriate' interactions of women and men, and egalitarian beliefs that are often spoken about. In our experience, we see that organizations are making determined efforts to eliminate conscious biases. As it becomes more politically incorrect and unacceptable to make statements on what is an appropriate job for a woman and what is not, many organizations are moving in a healthier direction. This does not, however, mean that the biases themselves have vanished. Sometimes, they have simply been pushed underground, and this makes them much harder to challenge or change.[4]

Off the record

Understanding the role gender plays makes you a far more compassionate manager.

Undervaluing women's work

Did you know that both men and women undervalue women's work? Surprised? Well, we were too. Let's take a look at the outcomes from an experiment in how gender impacts hiring decisions at Yale University.

Two hundred faculty members at the university were asked to evaluate an application from a senior undergraduate student applying for a job as lab manager. All the faculty participants received the same application, which was randomly assigned a male or female name. They were asked to judge the applicant's competency, how much they should be paid and whether or not they would be willing to mentor the student.

Somewhat depressingly, both men and women in the science faculty said that they were more likely to hire the male student, giving him higher ranks for competency and were willing to pay him $4,000 more than the woman. They were also more willing to mentor the male candidate than the female candidate.

What is remarkable is that this is an evaluation for suitability for an entry-level position, one where there is no reason to assume a woman or a man would be better suited for the role. This evaluation was done by well-accomplished men and women in science – not exactly what one has in mind when imagining ignorant and biased evaluators. In the real world, of course, we do not often have such well-designed experiments to make us aware of our unconscious biases. It slips by largely unnoticed, and instead gets explained away as a justified evaluation of competence.

Off the record

In India in particular, many women drop out of the organizational world in their 40s. Very few organizations have women in their 50s and 60s in senior roles.

Here's another interesting story about how unconscious bias works. Till 1970, women accounted for just 5 per cent of the musicians playing in leading US orchestras. In the 1970s and 1980s, many orchestras started the practice of conducting auditions from behind a curtain so that people selecting the musicians would hear only the music being played and not know who was playing it. Further, women were also instructed to remove their shoes before walking on to the stage so that the sound of their heels did not reveal their gender. This alone made it possible for the number of women musicians in these orchestras to go up to about 25–30 per cent.[5] It is proof of just how powerful unconscious biases are.

The important takeaway for us here is that unconscious biases exist and they affect women adversely. Awareness of these biases is the first and most important step in dealing with them and giving women the opportunities that they deserve.

Different standards of behaviour

For centuries, the standards for women's and men's behaviour have been vastly different. In the workplace, when women behave in the same manner as successful men, they tend to be less popular with both men and women employees. In what is now a famous demonstration of this effect, a professor from the Columbia Business School distributed to his students a case study on Heidi Roizen, a very successful Silicon Valley venture capitalist. However, some sections of his class received the same case study bearing the name Howard Roizen.[6]

The study dealt with how Heidi, a very successful networker, leverages her vast personal and professional network to build her business. Students were asked to rate Heidi (or Howard) Roizen on the bases of competence and likeability. While both Heidi and Howard were seen as competent, Heidi was liked far less. Further questioning of why Heidi didn't seem likeable revealed that she was seen as 'just not the sort of person you want to work with'. Her methods and success were seen as far too selfish for a woman. She had broken the largely unconscious expectation of assuming a nurturing, rather than aggressive, role.

It is clear that the success and likeability conundrum is not an easy one to crack for women. The behaviours that bring you popularity are often quite different from the ones that make you successful. While we seem to be more accepting when men make this trade-off, we find it harder to accept in women. There are no easy answers to this very fundamental dilemma. As Sheryl Sandberg states in *Lean In*, many successful women have developed a working style which is 'relentlessly positive'. Most successful women need to behave in a way that allows them to be very persistent about what they need to do while doing so with a smile.

Confidence challenges

To make things even more complex, we are now learning that there is a difference in the way men and women evaluate their own competence. Did you know that women tend to underplay their competence while men tend to overplay it. Understanding this difference is crucial to men and women working well together because it explains so much about what you see around you in the workplace.

Psychologist Zach Estes at the University of Milan has been studying this disparity in behaviour through a number of experiments.[7] In one experiment, 500 students attempted to reorganize a series of 3D spatial images on a computer. He found that the men in his study did far better than the women. When he re-examined the data on the answers, it turned out that these results were because women had attempted far fewer of the test questions. So, he conducted the experiment again, and he asked everyone to attempt all questions. This time round, the women did as well as the men on the test.

This reveals a crucial difference in the way men and women behave. Women seem to hesitate to do things that are unfamiliar to them. But once they try the unfamiliar, they actually perform as well as men. This is a very important difference to understand, because it helps us avoid mistaking hesitance for lack of competence. If you are a woman, you shouldn't be intimidated when you see the men in a room confidently assert they can do something you are hesitant about. Men and women simply seem to have different processing mechanisms. Similarly, if you are a man and see a woman appear timid, remember that her hesitance does not indicate lack of ability. She might have even performed that same task in the past. It simply comes down to different processing mechanisms.

We see these behaviours play out when job announcements are posted internally in an organization. Women tend to raise their hands for the job only if they meet 100 per cent of the criteria listed. On the other hand, men tend to raise their hands if they meet as much as 60 per cent of the criteria.[8] Quite often, women withhold because they hold themselves to much higher standards because of the expectations placed on them. Over the span of a career, such hesitance compounds and women become undervalued.

Claiming space

Another way unconscious bias plays out in the workplace is in the difference between how men and women claim, and are given, space in discussions. For instance, research shows that women are interrupted far more in meetings than men, and once interrupted, it is harder for women to get the floor back.[9] What's more, ideas put forward by men find it easier to gain traction than ideas put forward by women. For instance, a woman may find that an idea that she raised suddenly gets a lot of traction in a meeting because a male colleague has reiterated it.

Surprisingly, even women with experience and authority are not exempt from being interrupted. A study shows that women Supreme Court justices in the US are interrupted 3.9 times as much as their male colleagues, making it harder for them put forth their ideas and influence judgements.[10] Justice Ruth Bader Ginsburg has shared advice on how she deals with it, and part of this strategy has been to become more direct and assertive and not pay as much attention to the polite framing of her questions.[11] Of course, all of this happens without conscious intent. A lot of men and women mean well, and yet they operate with their own set of unconscious biases.

The difficulty in women claiming space sometimes manifests itself in physical spaces too. For instance, in crowded meeting rooms, women may automatically veer towards the back, while men automatically drift towards the centre. As a result, because of their physical location, their male colleagues can take centre stage. Hence, one of the things that women must learn fairly early on is how to claim space in meetings. They must also learn how to speak assertively so that their ideas are heard, thereby developing influence.

This may involve practising how to get the floor back when interrupted. Sometimes that could be as simple as saying, 'Would you mind if I finish first?' At other times, it may mean drawing attention back to your ideas by saying, 'Thank you for building on what I was saying.' You can say anything that works for you, but do remember to be assertive.

If you are a woman reading this chapter, and find that you have an idea that you would like to share, don't stay quiet at meetings. This does not call on one to be very aggressive, but just don't defer to everyone else simply because they were less thoughtful than you and didn't let you speak. If you are a man reading this chapter, we hope that this increased awareness of these issues will help you be more sensitive to the different ways in which you can create a more inclusive workplace.

In conclusion, in this chapter we have looked at the myriad reasons why men and women's careers often play out very differently in the organization, and what you can do to make the workplace more equal – whether you are a man or a woman. Truth be told, we are hopeful for the future as we see young women claim space more easily and see many men support the desire to build a more egalitarian workplace. The one thing we have ourselves seen time and again is that there is almost nothing that can stop a woman (or man) determined to make her (or his) mark in the world.

What You Can Do to Help Build a Level Playing Field

Challenge	What to do about it (If you are a woman)	What to do about it (If you are a man)
1. Explicit bias (stated biases that women are not suited for certain roles, either because the role is normally held by men or due to concerns regarding safety, etc.)	■ If you want that role, don't take no for an answer too soon. ■ Appreciate the concern, share your well-thought-out plans for what you will do in this role. Address any concerns you are aware of. ■ Be 'persistently pleasant' as you ask to be given the role. ■ If safety is a concern, think of what you and the organization can do to make this role safer. ■ When you get the opportunity, call out explicit biases politely and firmly.	■ Notice when explicit biases operate. They are sometimes phrased as being for the woman's own good. Call them out. ■ Do not assume that women will not be interested in certain roles. Always ask both men and women on your team about their interest. ■ Support your female colleagues as they try on roles that are new for them. They may often feel hesitant or even lonely without women role models to follow.

2. Undervaluing women's work (without consciously being aware)	■ Be aware that both men and women often undervalue work by women. Be conscious of how you judge other women. ■ Wherever possible, ask for measurable metrics. Where this is not possible, ask for examples of what doing a job well looks like. ■ Remember to communicate your accomplishments to others in the organization regularly, but do so sensitively. ■ Consciously and publicly appreciate good work done by other women in your team.	■ Be aware that both men and women often undervalue work done by women. Be conscious of how you judge work done by women. ■ Wherever possible, focus on measurable metrics and actual work outcomes for all members of your team equally. ■ Call out instances where you observe a woman's work not being valued equally. ■ Consciously and publicly appreciate good work done by the women (and men) in your team.
3. Hesitation to take on unfamiliar challenges	■ Be conscious of the fact that women hesitate more than men when they are faced with unfamiliar jobs.	■ Be conscious of the fact that women hesitate more than men when they consider unfamiliar jobs.

	■ When you are hesitant, question what your doubts actually are. ■ If the role is important, consciously build a learning map for yourself. Remember, spunk and courage are your friends. ■ If you are a manager, consciously tap women for new roles, and help them think through how they can do these well.	■ Being hesitant is no reflection of competence. ■ If you are a manager, consciously encourage women to take new roles and help them think through how they can do these well.
4. Being interrupted in meetings and or being hesitant to otherwise claim space in meetings	■ Ask yourself if this happens to you regularly. ■ Watch how other men and women claim space in meetings. This includes how they avoid being interrupted. Then practise, practise, practise holding on to your space.	■ Be conscious of when you are interrupting women in meetings. ■ If you absolutely need to interrupt, please give her the space back as soon as you have made your point, saying something along the lines of, 'I think you were saying something.'

	■ Whenever possible, give women space in meetings you are a part of. You can say something like, 'I think she was saying something.' ■ If you are a manager, make sure you ask the women in a meeting about their thoughts and ideas. For instance, you can say, 'Can we go around the table quickly to make sure everyone has shared their views?' Or you could ask individuals what they think at the end of the meeting.	■ If you are a manager, make sure you ask the women in the meeting about their thoughts and ideas. For instance, you can say, 'Can we go around the table quickly to make sure everyone has shared their views?' Or you could ask individuals what they think at the end of the meeting.
5. Hesitation to build a network at work	■ Remember, the best networks are built by your being the first to give support. Understanding that will make it easier for you to feel genuine about networking.	■ Be conscious of the fact that women sometimes hesitate to build networks. ■ Wherever it is natural and possible, integrate them into your networks.

	■ Remember that relationships built early in your career will last you a lifetime. So be very conscious and careful about developing a network. ■ Go out of your way to be helpful where you can. ■ Social chit-chat, exchanging news and views are natural elements of conversation. Feel comfortable to join these naturally. ■ If you are a manager, introduce women in your team to other senior leaders.	■ Be conscious when some of the social activities you are a part of, like going outside for a cigarette break or going out for post-work drinks, exclude women. ■ If you are a manager, introduce women in your team to other senior leaders and help them build a network. ■ Social chit-chat, exchanging news and views are natural elements of conversation. Be sure to include women in your conversations.

three

MANAGE

How well you understand yourself and how empowering your beliefs are will impact how you view your work and yourself. Reflect on important dimensions of your personality. Knowing yourself better will help you choose roles you will enjoy.

8

KNOW THYSELF

It is said that the words *gnothi seauton*, meaning 'know thyself', were once inscribed in the forecourt of the temple of Apollo at Delphi in ancient Greece. The oracle of Delphi was famous throughout the ancient world as the prescient predictor of future events, whose counsel was sought by rulers and citizens alike. Interestingly, people entering the temple to seek the wisdom of the oracle were urged to try and first know themselves before attempting to understand the outside world and future events.

There have also been many other famous uses of this phrase. Socrates, the ancient Greek philosopher, also used this maxim to urge people to delve deeper and understand themselves as a way to comprehend the world around them. A slightly different variation has been attributed to Lao Tzu, the Chinese philosopher, 'Mastering others is strength; mastering yourself is true power.'

If knowing yourself is power, then how can you gain this power? A little-known secret of organizational life is that successful leaders spend a lot of time, energy, effort and money to develop a deeper awareness of themselves and of the individuals on their team. This is especially important today because the world of business world is dynamic and constantly changing, and dealing with change requires adaptability. Knowing yourself well allows you to adapt better.

How we behave at work is influenced by the characteristics of our personalities, our habitual ways of behaving under stress and our key drivers and motivators (what we value in life). It is a fact that self-knowledge is a foundational skill for career success. If you can begin to understand who you really are, what you want from your career and how you are likely to behave in the workplace, you have a much better chance of being more effective and having a more fulfilling career. Unfortunately, these are not topics that are often talked about in undergraduate degree courses or business schools in India. In this chapter, we will discuss some basic questions and concepts about gaining greater self-awareness.

Personality, values and derailers

What do we mean by the word 'personality'? Personality is often defined as the characteristics or qualities of a person that make them a distinct individual. Personality matters because it creates predictable ways in which you are likely to behave at work. Sometimes, your personality will help you get ahead in your career, and sometimes it could get in the way. You may need to learn to behave in ways that don't come naturally or easily to you to be effective in your organization.

For example, you may be a very systematic and organized person. If you work as a project manager, this aspect of your personality will really help you. However, if you are working as a project manager in a start-up environment where things tend to be fairly chaotic, learning to live with the chaos will not come easily to you. Knowing someone's personality also matters because it helps you understand why your co-workers behave the way they do and how you might need to adapt to work more effectively with them.

What are values? A useful definition of values is that they are the beliefs that we consider important in life. What you consider as important will be what you will focus on. For example, if you value connecting with people, you will focus on building relationships. You will also try to achieve what you value. For instance, if you value money, you will work hard to earn money. You will find that organizational culture is influenced by the values of the founders, senior leaders and employees who choose to work with the organization, and that often, they have a shared set of values.

Finally, derailers are negative behaviours that you may display when you are under stress. We are seldom at our best behaviour when under stress, and our behaviours erode in the most predictable fashion. Road rage is an extreme example of how even the nicest of people you know can turn into 'beasts' under extreme stress caused by traffic. When derailers remain unmanaged, these aspects of our behaviour can often create performance risks for us. These behaviours are also referred to as the 'dark side' of personality. Let us begin by looking at personality characteristics that are known to impact workplace behaviours the most.

The Big Five personality traits

After years of research, psychologists in the US have arrived at a set of attributes called the Big Five personality traits.[1] These are the five qualities within you that have the most impact on how you are likely to behave at work. These Big Five characteristics are seen across all cultures, countries and socio-economic backgrounds, and it is a model that is often used to describe human personality and workplace behaviours.

It is also referred to as the five factor model (FFM), and the acronym OCEAN is an easy way to remember these five attributes.

O: Openness to experience
C: Conscientiousness
E: Extraversion
A: Agreeableness
N: Neuroticism (emotional stability)

Standardized personality assessments were developed to measure people on these personality dimensions. Among the well-researched, scientific measures of Big Five personality dimensions are the Hogan Personality Inventory and the HEXACO. Personality assessments are used in the workplace to build increased self-awareness. They are also used during hiring to assess job fit.

Depending on how high or low you score on each of the Big Five attributes, you are likely to behave in certain ways, and depending on what traits are required to do your job, your personality will either help or hinder your performance. Let's try and understand these five dimensions to see how you are likely to score on each of them.

Openness to experience

If you are generally curious, creative, full of ideas and willing to try new things, then you are probably high on the openness attribute. People who have a higher degree of the openness attribute are also likely to get easily bored, especially with routine or repetitive work. So if you don't need too much change or variety and don't get bored easily, you may be lower on the openness attribute. As a result, you may also be a lot more practical, pragmatic and able to complete routine or operational work. The flipside to this is that experimentation or trying new ways of doing things may not come easily to you, even when the old ways of working require change.

How does this matter? Well, early in your career, there are limited opportunities to display creativity or strategic thinking. Your job roles will tend to be more operational in nature or you will be expected to mostly follow orders. In this scenario, having a lower score on openness may help you. As someone who has a high degree of openness to experience, following orders and being tactical or operational may be somewhat difficult for you. Our advice is to be patient. Almost every job has a routine and mundane aspect. Building tolerance for these aspects of any job will be useful throughout your life. Your focus should be to gain experience and show that you can be relied upon to get things done.

The next attribute of conscientiousness will certainly help you build a reputation of someone who is reliable and gets things done.

Conscientiousness

If you are generally organized, detail-oriented and good at following through with plans, you are probably higher on the conscientiousness dimension. This attribute will help you create a reputation for being reliable and trustworthy. However, you should be careful to not overdo the planning and to show flexibility when plans change. If being flexible when plans change on short notice does not come easily to you, people may begin to see you as somewhat inflexible or rigid, especially when it comes to plans, processes and rules.

On the other hand, people ranked lower on the conscientiousness dimension, tend to be a lot more flexible, adaptable and do not need much structure. During personal or professional upheaval, people with lower scores on conscientiousness are likely to find it easier to adapt to the change. On the flipside, their lack of disciple and attention to detail may sometimes create a reputation for being unreliable. If they don't pay attention, they are likely to miss deadlines and not follow through on commitments.

India is a country of contradictions. Being overly organized doesn't necessarily work here because we are challenged on an almost daily basis to adapt, change and remain flexible. Find your balance between rigidly sticking to a plan and remaining flexible. The reputation that you are trying to build is one of being a reliable, trustworthy colleague who gets the job done. Every company has its own norms about which employee is seen as more reliable. You may agree or disagree with these norms, but they do exist, and it is best to figure them out and begin to build a reputation of being reliable. Sometimes, it is as simple as arriving on time and checking with people before leaving from work.

Openness and conscientiousness are about how you do your work. How you relate to others is equally important and the next two personality attributes – extraversion and agreeableness – will determine your approach to building relations.

Extraversion

Extraversion is about connecting with the external world around us. Those who are high on extraversion enjoy interacting with people. They are often outgoing, talkative, and find it easy to connect with new people. They also tend to know many people and seem to have a large network of friends, acquaintances and professional contacts. Because of their tendency to talk more than listen, they may come across as distracted or as poor listeners.

Those who are lower on the extraversion dimension tend to have a reputation of being good listeners. That's because they tend to talk less and are quieter, as a result of which, they seem to listen well to others. Because they tend to hold back from social interactions, they may have a limited network of friends, acquaintances or professional contacts.

If talking to people at and outside work comes easily to you, you are probably higher on extraversion. You can use this strength to start building a network of relationships that will be helpful even later in life. However, watch out for the tendency to get distracted. If you score lower on extraversion, you may need to develop your ability to have conversations and make small talk. These skills will be useful to you throughout your career because a big part of corporate life is interacting with other people: peers, clients, vendor partners, managers.

While extraversion drives the frequency of social interaction, agreeableness determines how rewarding others will find their interactions with you.

Agreeableness

Agreeableness is the extent to which a person comes across as warm, friendly and considerate towards others. Those who score high on agreeableness are easy-going, caring and sensitive in interpersonal communication. However, these people tend to find it difficult to deal with conflict or give critical feedback. Those who score lower on the agreeableness dimension tend to be quite direct, forthright and candid. They may also come across as blunt and lacking tact.

Having a higher degree of agreeableness will make it easier for others to connect with you. You will, however, need to build the skills required to deal with conflict. If you are lower on agreeableness, others may find it difficult to connect with you. So watch out for that tendency to be blunt, and be careful about what you say.

There are certainly regional stereotypes that operate in India about the parts of the country from which people are likely to be more or less agreeable. Pradnya is from Maharashtra, and she often jokes that Maharashtrians have to remind themselves each year on Makar Sankranti to speak sweetly. On this day, Maharashtrians give each other *til* (sesame) and gur (jaggery) laddus and wish each other by saying '*Til-gul ghya ani god-god bola!*' ('Please eat some sesame and jaggery and let's speak sweetly to each other!')

But more than regional differences, organizational cultures will fall somewhat more or less on this dimension. Being nice and considerate may be a virtue in one organization and quite the opposite in another. Pay attention to this, try to understand where you are likely to be on this scale and learn to adapt when required.

Neuroticism

Neuroticism is typically defined as a tendency towards anxiety, self-doubt, depression, shyness and other similar negative feelings. Since all personality traits, including emotional instability, exist on a spectrum, everyone is a little neurotic to some degree. Sigmund Freud, the famous psychoanalyst, used to say that all human beings are somewhat neurotic. While this is not necessarily true, the dimension of neuroticism or emotional stability does significantly impact workplace performance. People scoring low on the neuroticism scale come across as calm, composed and even-tempered. Their calmness, especially when a sense of urgency is required, can create a misleading reputation of being nonchalant or unresponsive.

> **Off the record**
>
> At job interviews you might be asked to complete a personality assessment. Don't try to second-guess what the employers are looking for, and answer as honestly as you can. Getting a job where you will be a misfit is both painful and a waste of time.

On the other hand, those scoring high on the neuroticism dimension work with a sense of urgency. They are careful about not making mistakes, are watchful for things going wrong and tend to be open to feedback. They also tend to be a lot more anxious, self-critical, and may worry too much. They may seem moody, temperamental or irritable and may not trust people easily. These characteristics combined with their anxiety and moodiness can get in the way of building strong relationships at work.

If you are prone to anxiety, you should start building emotional resilience and find a way to not take on a lot of stress. Meditation, mindfulness, regular exercise, cultivating hobbies and interests beyond work and spending time with people that you like are important stress busters. Eating healthy and getting plenty of rest is also equally important. If you build these habits early in your career they will serve you well throughout your life and help mitigate any risks associated with work-related stress and anxiety.

Remember that there is no good or bad personality. Your personality is a natural part of who you are. What matters is your ability to understand yourself and adapt your behaviour in order to be even more productive and build effective workplace relationships. Along with your personality, your values, and specifically what you value at work, also influence how you work. More importantly, your values will often influence whether you are happy or unhappy with your job or organization. It is a fact that we like to work with people who share our values and are happiest in work environments that are consistent with our values.

Workplace values

Psychologists Robert and Joyce Hogan, well-known personality psychologists from the US, have created a useful taxonomy of 10 workplace values that seem to motivate workplace behaviours and determine whether people are likely to feel happy and satisfied with their work and organization. They built a standardized assessment known as the Motives, Values and Preferences Inventory (MVPI)[2] to assess how people in an organization scored on each of these values.

This is the list of the 10 workplace values as proposed by the Hogans:

1. Recognition: interested in fame and public recognition
2. Power: enjoying status, career advancement, creating impact
3. Hedonism: having fun, enjoying life, valuing work-life balance
4. Altruistic: desirous of helping others
5. Affiliation: desirous of connecting with others
6. Tradition: having a strong sense of right and wrong
7. Security: valuing stability and predictability
8. Commerce: interested in business, commerce and making money
9. Aesthetics: valuing creativity, art and self-expression
10. Science: valuing analysis and problem solving

1. Recognition: Those who value recognition are motivated by public recognition and prefer to work in environments that provide them opportunities to be recognized by their colleagues and the general public.

2. Power: Those motivated by power enjoy high status, desire career advancement and want to create an impact. They like working in high-achievement, competitive environments that give them the opportunity to advance in their career and make an impact.

3. **Hedonism:** The principle of hedonism is about having fun and enjoying yourself. Those motivated by hedonism seek variety, excitement and pleasure. They like to work in environments that allow for travel, entertainment, good food and drink, fun and informality. 'Work hard and play hard' is a mantra they seem to live by.

4. **Altruistic:** Being altruistic is about helping others. Those who value being altruistic are drawn to professions and careers in which they can help others. They value teamwork and are always willing to help others at their workplace. They fail to understand people who don't want to help their teammates. They enjoy working in organizations that are employee-friendly and look after their people.

5. **Affiliation:** This value is about connecting with people. People who value affiliation like to meet and build relations with others. They also like working in teams because they enjoy team interactions.

6. **Tradition:** This value is about conservatism. People who are drawn to this value will typically have conservative ideas and will work best in environments that seem fair and just, and which value traditions.

7. **Security:** Security is all about stability and avoiding undue risk. Individuals who score highly on the security scale like to minimize risk. They like stable work environments, large stable companies and predictable work.

8. Commerce: Commerce is an interest in making money. People who value commerce highly will enjoy doing business, and they will likely remain focused on the bottom line. Organizations that are numbers-driven and which remain focused on top- and bottom-line results are the places in which they will be the happiest.

9. Aesthetics: This value is about putting an emphasis on creativity. High-aesthetics individuals will enjoy design, creativity and will seek opportunities for self-expression in their work. They are also very concerned about the look and feel of things and will spend large amounts of money to make something look good. Organizations that put value on style and good taste will be their preferred places to work.

10. Science: People who value science have a deep interest in science, technology, data and logical thinking. They are rational, logical thinkers and they need data to make decisions.

Now that you have a basic understanding of Hogan's 10 workplace values, try to determine which values are more important to you because these will drive your workplace behaviours. Ask yourself if there is a good fit between your values and your role and your organization. Are you able to find expression for or satisfaction with your higher values?

When your values are aligned with those of your organization, you will feel satisfied with your job and find it easier to be productive. If you value achievement and success, and are working for a company that is competitive and driven to achievement, you will find that the environment is a good fit for you. If you enjoy helping others, you will be happier in a job that requires serving customers.

When there is a mismatch between what you value and what the organization considers important, or what is required for the job, it can create dissatisfaction. A mismatch of values is often the root cause for people feeling unhappy with their job or choosing to leave an organization. For example, if you value achievement, fast growth and taking on big goals but are working at a well-established company where the level of ambition and aspiration is not that high, you may soon begin to feel frustrated.

If you discover that some of your key values are not being met in your current role or the organization, try and find expression for them outside work. You could also reflect on what you may need to do differently to satisfy the value. For example, to earn recognition or power, you would need to take initiative, show effective performance and create visibility for your work. Think carefully about how you can make this happen and then seek those opportunities at your workplace.

If you have too many values that you prize equally, it would be very difficult for all of them to be met at any one time by any one organization or job. In that case, you may have to prioritize your values. For example, your values of hedonism or aesthetics may not be met in a workplace that is scientific, analytical and technical, where most of your colleagues tend to be serious and happier working alone. You could try to meet your need for hedonism outside the workplace. Do things you enjoy or after work, because this is an important aspect of your life.

Another thing to observe is whether what you value is also supported by how you behave on a day-to-day basis as reflected in your Big Five personality dimensions. For example, if you score highly on affiliation, which is a desire to connect with others, do you also show extraversion in your behaviours? If you are an altruistic personality, are you also demonstrating agreeableness, and exhibit behaviours that demonstrate sensitivity towards others? If you value commerce, power or recognition, are you also demonstrating behaviours associated with achievement and ambition, which are behaviours associated with both extraversion and conscientiousness?

Our values also create strong, unconscious biases within us. Most people assume that others share their values, and we tend to like people who are like us. As a result, you may find it difficult to get along with people whose values are very different from yours. Being aware of your biases and why you find it easy or difficult to get along with someone will help you build effective working relationships at work.

We've now looked at the Big Five personality variables and values and how they are likely to influence your behaviour at work under normal circumstances. However, when we are stressed out, we often tend to behave in ways that are different from our day-to-day behaviours.

Derailers

When you see or hear about extremely smart and successful people saying or doing extremely silly things, it's probably their under-stress personality showing up in an unmanaged way. Corporate life is full of stress and challenges, and when we are stressed out, our psychological defence mechanisms begin to engage to help us cope with the stress and reduce our anxiety. These defence mechanisms are mostly unconscious, habitual patterns of behaviour. They have served us well in the past and this is what leads to them being overused.

Coping mechanisms are related to the 'dark side' of our personality – characteristics that help, but also hinder performance when over-used. Robert and Joyce Hogan also studied the dark side traits and their derailing aspects that can create performance risks. Drawing from the work of psychoanalyst Karen Horney and referencing other personality research, the Hogans defined 11 dimensions of behaviour that create derailment risks under stress.

These 11 dimensions can be grouped into three themes that seem to emerge when people are trying to cope with workplace stress and interpersonal conflicts. Let's take a look at these three themes and associated 11 dark-side traits.

Hogan taxonomy of under-stress behaviours[3]

1. Moving away: behaviours that tend to push others away
2. Moving against: behaviours aimed at trying to control, manipulate or dominate others
3. Moving towards: behaviours directed towards seeking alignment or building alliances

1. Moving Away: These behaviours show up as emotional volatility, including feeling disappointed and giving up easily on people or projects (excitable); becoming suspicious and mistrustful of others or displaying general cynicism (sceptical); becoming withdrawn, cold and aloof (reserved); becoming overly cautious and not taking action (cautious); becoming stubborn or saying one thing but not following through with action (leisurely).

If you do not control these behaviours, and they remain unmanaged, moving-away behaviours can make it difficult for you to build strong partnerships with others. You may then begin to appear temperamental, distrusting, uncooperative or aloof and withdrawn to your colleagues.

2. Moving Against: These behaviours show up in a variety of ways such as being assertive to the point of aggression (bold), being overly charming to get other people to support your agendas (mischievous) or by becoming overly dramatic to make your point (colourful). Sometimes, these behaviours may manifest as throwing in multiple ideas in order to win people over (imaginative); however, it can often leave others feeling overwhelmed. Overusing moving-against behaviours could impact your reputation negatively as others may see you as being unable to acknowledge your shortcomings, only wanting to have your own way and not making an effort to reach a middle ground.

3. Moving Towards: These behaviours manifest themselves when you try to build alliances by being overly pleasing and deferential (dutiful) or by being overly hardworking or perfectionistic (diligent). The overuse of moving-towards behaviours creates the risk of being seen as being someone who is nitpicky or unable to hold an independent perspective.

These under-stress behaviours are mostly unconscious, and you may not even be aware of their negative impact. All of these behaviours allow you to cope effectively with work stress and interpersonal conflicts. For example, cautious leaders are generally careful and considerate in making decisions, even under stress. This allows them to make better decisions. Or excitable behaviours can show people what you are passionate or

Off the record

Moving against behaviours are geared to get one's own way and thus drive achievement. Moving away behaviours have a more consistently negative impact on workplace success. Managing both is important for success.

enthusiastic about. However, the word we must focus on in these definitions is 'overly'. Overdoing any of these 11 behaviours can get in the way of effective performance. When we pay attention to our behaviours, it is easier to tone down or manage the overuse of any of these coping mechanisms. There are several ways in which you can learn to regulate and manage your derailing behaviours. Let's take a look at a few of these ways.

Self-management

Marshall Goldsmith is a leadership development expert who has simplified the challenge of managing the self at the workplace to managing how you are sharing or withholding information and emotion. In his bestselling book *What Got You Here Won't Get You There*, he adds the dimension of 'appropriateness' to sharing or withholding of information.[4]

In the workplace, we are constantly interacting with others, and Goldsmith recommends that when sharing information or emotions you need to ask yourself two questions: Is sharing this information/emotion appropriate? If it is, how much should I share with my colleague? Especially in times of stress, pausing to answer these questions will help you stay in a safe zone and avoid getting derailed.

Workplace stress is almost always caused either by situations outside your control or by the people you need to work with.

All workplace interactions generate an emotional reaction in us. Social interactions almost always require some exchange of information, and this often causes many of us to approach such situations with a degree of caution.

Three Questions for Effective Self-Management

1. What am I feeling?
2. Can I share what I am feeling?
3. How much should I share?

(Adapted from Marshall Goldsmith)

The first step to resolving this situation is to acknowledge that you are having an emotional reaction and labelling that reaction. For example, you could say that you are feeling angry, annoyed, irritated, hurt, upset, frustrated or overwhelmed. When you are in the grip of a powerful emotion, asking yourself how much of your emotions you should show and whether it appropriate to share your emotions helps calibrate your emotional reactivity.

Similarly, in any situations where there is an exchange of information, check yourself to determine if you are sharing too much, too little or just the right amount of information. Also, you should also check if the information you are sharing can be shared with the concerned person(s) or whether you need to be more discreet. If you are not sure, check with your manager. In general, information that will help someone can almost always be shared openly. It's when the information is likely to be damaging to a person or the organization or is likely to hurt someone that you need to be especially careful.

Our personality drives habitual, unconscious behaviours. Our behaviours can be perceived by others positively or negatively, thus either helping or hindering our performance at work. How our behaviours are perceived by others builds our reputation. Reputation is what others think of us while identity is what we think of ourselves.

Identity versus reputation

There are two ways of thinking about one's personality. The first is what you see from within – the individual's view of their personality. This is your identity. The second is from the point of view of others, or the observer's view of an individual's personality. This is your reputation.

While identity is important, it is equally, and sometimes more, important to understand what others think of you at the workplace. We know that self-aware leaders solicit feedback, accept it and adapt their behaviours to better a workplace situation for themselves and their organization. They actively manage their reputations.

On the other hand, those who lack self-awareness shy away from feedback, ignore or overlook the feedback and seldom act on it. Eventually, such individuals plateau in their career growth or even experience career derailment.

Now that you are armed with useful frameworks to start thinking about what drives your workplace behaviours, and how you can be more effective and productive, let's begin to look at what drives long-term career success.

RAW talent

Most organizations usually define workplace competencies, and these are what is required to be successful in the organization or at a particular role within the organization. Competencies can be defined as a set of knowledge, skills, abilities and other personality characteristics that allow you to perform successfully. In his book *The Talent Delusion*, Tomas Chamorro-Premuzic posits that all competency models can be reduced to three fundamental buckets of talent, and he calls it the RAW model of talent.[5]

The RAW model is a little-known secret in organizations and is a useful model to focus on as you chart your own journey to career success. In this model, R stands for rewarding, A for able and W for willing. Successful people tend to have a lot of RAW talent, that is, they tend to be rewarding to work with, able to do the job and willing to put in the effort to do the job.

Rewarding

A person's likeability determines how rewarding they are to work with. Other parameters remaining the same, likeable people demonstrate well-developed interpersonal skills and a greater ability to manage their emotional outbursts, making it more likely that they bevome successful.

Able

Success also depends on expertise or your ability to do a job. No one is born knowing everything, but it is important to ensure that you either possess or build the expertise needed to perform in your job. Ability is thus the second factor critical to career success.

Willing

The third and factor for career success is your willingness or the motivation to work hard. Your development also depends on how much effort you are willing to put in to learn and grow, and achieve your goals.

The RAW model is another useful framework to keep in mind as you build your corporate career. Building careers is hard work. In today's dynamic, changing world of work, you do need a life-long commitment to learning, as ability is forever being stretched and tested. And it's not enough that you know how to do the job. You have to be willing to put in the effort and do the work. Finally, in general, people like to work with people they like. We are not suggesting that you become fake or ingratiating. Being a rewarding person is making an effort to be interpersonally sensitive and managing your emotionality at the workplace.

Observing yourself in action, reflecting on your behaviours and their outcomes and asking people you trust for feedback on how you are doing are great ways to continue to build personal effectiveness. It is equally important to make sure that you are taking the time to recover from the daily work-life stress.

Practising recovery

Living in the modern world is by itself stressful, and constant changes and transitions in the workplace add to this stress. A good habit to inculcate early in your career is the practice of recovering from stress at the workplace. For example, professional athletes always build recovery time into their training schedule to be able to keep up with the rigours of their sport. Similarly, it is important to build recovery practices into your daily life. Hobbies, spending time with friends and family and weekend vacations are all great stress busters. Building a daily routine of exercise is another way in which you can build resilience to deal with stress.

Mindfulness meditation is a special recovery technique that you can make into a regular habit. Mindfulness requires you to sit quietly, focus on your breath as a means to calm to your mind and observe your thoughts without being derailed by them. Building a regular mindfulness practice will help you calm your mind in times of stress and react to situations appropriately.

Personal effectiveness

These three personal effectiveness principles will serve you well on your journey to building a long and successful corporate career:

1. **Reflection:** Build the practice of watching yourself in action and reflecting on your actions, their impact, and if you could've done anything differently in a situation. Reflection – action – reflection can be the rhythm for your personal growth and development.

2. **Seeking feedback:** Spend time understanding your personality, motivations and coping mechanisms. Seek feedback from others on your behaviours to validate your own understanding of yourself.

3. Practicing recovery: Even as you work hard, take the time out for recovery. Like athletes, recovery is important for sustained high performance. Emotional resilience helps manage behaviours under stress and reduce the risks of derailment.

Building careers means experiencing change. Sometimes the change is initiated by you, such as a new role, a new organization or a new city. At other times, the change is imposed on you, such as a company reorganization that leads to a change in the manager or the team, or change in a critical work process, your manager leaving, your project being terminated, and many more. Your ability to deal effectively with change will enable smoother, less stressful transitions.

Tips and Takeaways

- Understanding yourself helps with adaptability which in turn drives success.
- Under stress we often over react, and this leads to derailment. Our reactions are predictable, and understanding can help us manage these behaviours.
- Self-management is to know what, when and how much to share.
- Identity is what we think of ourselves; reputation is what others think of us. Our personality drives our behaviour. Our behaviour, as perceived by others, leads to our reputation.

9

EMBRACE CHANGE

Anushri (name changed) graduated with an MBA in Human Resources from a reputed institute in Delhi. She reached out to her network and found a job with a small consulting company. She enjoyed the work and the people she worked with, but her office was at a distance from her home. The commute was over an hour long and Anushri was always late for work. This began to impact her reputation with her bosses and her peers. Whenever there was a discussion about individuals ready for more responsibility, the conversation would always circle back to how she was always late for work. Could she be trusted to take on more responsibility? Would she deliver on time?

As students we have a lot of flexibility with our time because our schedules are designed by us. But when we start working, we are expected to show up every day at a certain time. Whether we like it or not, people are watching what time we come to work and what time we leave the office and making judgements about our work ethic based on these timings. Our co-workers, clients, bosses are also depending on the predictability of our timings. Being on time for work, on a daily basis, is the first reality of transition to work.

Embracing this reality is often a difficult transition for most people when they first start working.

You may wonder why it was so difficult for Anushri to be on time. After all, wouldn't it just need a small adjustment to her routine? But Anushri's inability to embrace her new reality lay at the heart of the problem – that she was expected to show up at a certain time every day without fail. When you don't show up on time, whether to office or a meeting outside, people begin to doubt your commitment to work.

In this chapter, we will discuss shifting gears from student life to corporate life. We will talk about some of the changes and challenges you will encounter as you make this transition. Change and transitions will continue throughout your career, and the ideas and strategies that we discuss here will help you deal with future change and transitions. We will also share stories that may resonate with you and help you realize that you are not alone in what you may be feeling or experiencing.

Reality bites

Most times, you will begin a new job with a lot of aspiration and expectations. Sometimes the actual work will be to your liking and sometimes it won't. Sometimes your colleagues and work conditions will be supportive, and sometimes they won't. This is when reality hits.

Let's take the example of Rhea (name changed). She graduated at the top of her class in her master's degree in economics from Jawaharlal Nehru University (JNU). She was hired as a business analyst by a leading financial ratings company, and after the initial induction period was over, Rhea began to feel quite frustrated with her work. When she was hired, she was told that she would be working on interesting and exciting projects with very senior consultants from whom she could learn and grow. However, she soon realized that many of her projects were similar. And the seniors she was looking forward to learning from were actually too busy to mentor her or give her new, challenging assignments. A lot of her time was being spent in data collection and entry, and she was thoroughly bored. Rhea was ready to find a new job.

It is not uncommon to have a picture in your mind about what work will be like, only to discover that it is, in fact, quite different from reality. It's a bit like the difference between a movie trailer and the actual movie. Based on the trailer, each one of us has an idea of what to expect, and that is what drives us into the hall. But sometimes, the trailer has all the good parts of the movie, while at other times the movie completely outdoes the trailer.

Similarly, you probably have a picture in your mind created both by what you were told and the hopes in your mind about what your new job will be like. This is what happened in Rhea's case. Has this happened to you? Have you come to understand, and most importantly accept, that most jobs also have very mundane, boring, monotonous aspects that are equally important?

Vipul (name changed), the Indian managing director of a multinational pharmaceutical company, shared his first 'embracing reality' experience with us. About 25 years ago,

Vipul was hired as a member of the field sales team of a large, multinational pharmaceutical company in Hyderabad. He was fresh out of college, and had been given targets that he thought were unrealistic. His manager was based in Chennai and had never worked in the Hyderabad market.

Vipul got very little support from his manager, although he states that he didn't have any obstruction from the manager either. The manager basically left him alone to do whatever he could in the market. In the beginning, Vipul felt angry at his boss and at the company. He wanted to do well but with no one to guide him, he began to feel frustrated and started thinking of quitting or looking for another job. But there was no guarantee that life would be any better in the next job.

Vipul forced himself to get past these feelings and decided to first try doing whatever he could in his current job before quitting and moving on. He reached out to other colleagues in field sales who were responsible for other products to see what they were doing. He accompanied them on their sales calls. If they made three calls a day, he would go to all three and then make three calls for his own products. He would spend as much time in the market as he could, meeting people and talking to anyone who was willing to talk to him. Vipul had grown up in Mumbai. He had never lived in Hyderabad. He did not know the local language and was not familiar with the local culture and customs. He found that he had to get used to a new city, new language and new culture.

But soon, through his market visits, Vipul began to understand his customers better. Along the way, he picked up spoken Telugu and built a large local network. Within six months, Vipul was not only doing very well, but he had also begun to invite his manager from Chennai to introduce him around the Hyderabad market. Today, he tells this story to young recruits that his company hires from colleges. 'Life is what you make of it' is his motto.

Once you decide to accept your new reality, you can then begin the process of adapting to your new company and culture. This begins with trying to understand the organization that you have joined. The first few months of a new job are invaluable while trying to understand your organization.

Learning on the job

Perhaps you suspect this already, but when you join a new organization or even take on a new role within your existing organization, there is a period of learning and proving yourself. People are watching what you are doing and how you are working. It is often only after you have earned their trust that you begin to get greater responsibilities and interesting work. You can use this learning period to observe what is happening around you, how your organization works and perhaps even to see how other organizations are driven. This is perhaps the time to listen carefully to what is being said by your managers and other leaders to begin to understand the vision and business goals.

Quarterly Earnings Calls

Most publicly listed companies will have a quarterly earnings call for analysts. Earning calls are conference calls between the management of a company, financial analysts, investors and media to discuss the company's financial performance

> during a reporting period. While these calls are not required by law, more and more companies are having these calls. These calls are open to public. Most companies record and post these calls on their websites for anyone to listen to. Call transcripts are also often published online. Listening to the most recent earnings call will give you further understanding into the company financials, current performance and future goals. You will also hear how your CEO and CFO present themselves and the company.

The insights into organizations you develop at this time will go a long way in making better decisions about how you build your career. You will learn to understand the current challenges, opportunities and concerns for leaders in your organization.

From understanding business strategy and financials, let's turn our attention to the mundane, everyday work life around you and how you can continue to learn more about the company and people by just being more observant. For instance, how do people dress at your new company? Thinking about dress codes may seem frivolous, but another well-kept secret of organizations is that people in an organization do tend to dress alike. There is a distinct style of dressing that you will be able to discern. For example, when one of the authors, Pradnya, worked at Microsoft, she felt completely overdressed in her silk and cotton sarees. Soon, she adopted a more informal dressing style.

Pay attention to how people are dressing in the roles that you wish to rise to, and within your budget and aligned with your own aesthetics you can also adopt a tone of dressing. Dress for the job you desire or levels you wish to rise to and not necessarily the job you have. Even as you are observing and learning about things within your organization, if your new job has taken you to a new city or a new region, there is often a lot of learning and adjusting you may need to do to adapt to regional differences.

Regional differences

In addition to changes in role or differences in organizational context, external cultural differences can also have a significant impact in India, especially from one state to another. Language is often the most obvious difference that you will deal with. However, in a sales role, spending time in the field will help you learn the language and begin to understand your customers faster. This is exactly what Vipul did when he was posted to Hyderabad for his first job.

Although lifestyles in most urban cities in India are becoming increasingly similar, there are still noticeable differences between regions. People moving from any other part of India to Mumbai often find it overwhelmingly crowded. Shops open by 8 a.m. or 8.30 a.m. in Mumbai, and local eateries like Udupi restaurants start serving breakfast as early as 6 a.m. This is unheard of in a place like Delhi, where shops don't open until after 10 a.m.

There are often regional differences in the pace at which people work, the manner in which they speak and relate to each other at work and what is considered appropriate and inappropriate behaviour. And if you have primarily lived in large, urban spaces, the first time you move to a smaller town or a rural setting will possibly find you feeling uncomfortable. The reverse is also true – if you have primarily lived in smaller towns or rural areas, the pace, crowds, pollution and other aspects of living in urban cities will definitely be challenging. There may also be regional differences in dressing styles – some dictated by the weather and some by custom. For example, in Delhi, people have a separate summer and winter wardrobe.

As you move to a new place, you will need to make these observation in order to be able to adapt. Of course, because you are used to things being a certain way, these differences may seem uncomfortable, annoying or even stressful in the beginning. Over time, and sometimes with some effort, you *will* adapt and may even start enjoying your new life. Getting used to all changes often require, what is known as, a period of transition. Transition is the internal process of adaptation to the changes around you within the organization and sometimes outside the organization. While this has a tendency to throw us off, often, the ability to bounce back is an important one that we should cultivate.

Managing transitions

William Bridges is a researcher who has done a lot of work in the area of change and transition. His book *Managing Transitions* was published over 25 years ago, and in it he talks about transition as the inner psychological process of coming to terms with the changes around us. Embracing our new realities and allowing new beliefs and behaviours to emerge is the inner psychological process that Bridges is talking about. Change is external to us – such as a new role, new place of work, a new manager, a new city, a new performance appraisal system and so on. Bridges refers to the internal process of adaptation to this change as transition.

Paradoxically, every transition begins with an ending – an end to a way of life. What follows is what Bridges calls a neutral zone, when you are adapting to your new reality. You may experience strong emotional reactions during this time including stress and anxiety. Vipul experienced strong negative emotions during his transition to working in Hyderabad. As Vipul says, 'I first got angry and I felt sad, and then I just decided to keep at it and learn from whoever and whatever was happening around me.' However, as you gain understanding about your altered reality, new beliefs and behaviours emerge and there is now a beginning. These new beginnings release energy and people are reoriented and renewed.

It is true that change brings with it stress and anxiety. This is the nature of change and the human condition. Even when the change is positive and by your choice, you will still feel the stress and anxiety. You will feel anxious to do well, learn and contribute to your work environment. Let's call this positive stress, and this will fuel and energize you. When the change is not to your liking, the stress and anxiety is far more pronounced, and it is often quite negative.

All of us go through an intense period of adjustment or readjustment to new realities. People seldom talk about it, because once the period is past and you assimilate into the new reality, this period is usually forgotten. You may have experienced this earlier when you first stepped away from the warm comfort of home to a college hostel. Or perhaps in an earlier job? If you are at your very first job, your stress is no surprise at all.

This stress will happen when you change jobs, or take on a new role, when new team members join your team or when you get a new manager. This stress will happen every time there is any change in your life and your work situation. Depending on the degree of change, your emotional reactions will be more or less intense. Under conditions of negative stress, human beings are hardwired to react with the 'fight, flight or freeze' responses. At the workplace, this plays out as a strong desire to quit or try to go back to an earlier role where you were comfortable (flight), becoming angry or frustrated (fight) or feeling sad and helpless to do anything (freeze).

Vipul shared another experience of a major career transition that he had to live through many years later. He had risen rapidly through the ranks and been promoted to an international role, following which he moved with his wife and young daughter to Singapore. Less than a year into this role, his company underwent a major reorganization and as a part of this, Vipul's role was eliminated. He was naturally quite upset by this turn of events. However, with his motto of 'Life is what you make of it', he decided once again not to give in to his emotions but to embrace this new reality instead. Looking for a job became his new job, and he dedicated himself to that role with the same commitment that he had always had for his work.

Off the record

The law of inertia seems to operate in humans as well, and maintaining the status quo is often the most desired state. To resist change is human. Keep this in mind when you are trying to influence others to change.

He would get up in the morning, get ready, as if going to work, and start his new 'job'. He made a list of all the people he had ever connected with in his work life and systematically started reaching out to them. He told them very directly that his role had been eliminated and he was looking to find another role. He updated his résumé, and set up meetings and phone calls. While some days were better than others, and the going was not easy, he persisted. He kept himself open to all opportunities and it took three long months of hard work and focus before he managed to find himself a role at a higher level back in India.

You can learn several lessons from these stories and put them into practice to overcome the pitfalls of managing career transitions.

Understand your emotions

To be human is to experience stress at different times of life. And our human brain has a rather frustrating response to stress. Stress activates the oldest part of our brain – the limbic system – and shuts off the part of the brain that we most prize – our ability to be thoughtful and make good judgement calls. Just when we need our judgement the most, it vanishes. And that sucks. But being aware that you are stressed makes it possible for you to do something about it. Like Vipul, commit to embracing your new reality and giving it your best shot to quickly adapt to your changing situation.

Learn to let go

Change requires us to let go of our familiar, comfortable ways of behaving. That's fundamentally what makes change difficult. Hence, you should learn to let go of habits that don't seem to serve you well in the new situation. For Anushri, perhaps the leisurely pace of her mornings was one habit she needed to change the most to make it on time to work. For Rhea, perhaps letting go of her expectations of what the job ought to have been and instead, doing her best with the job that was assigned to her would be the most effective way forward.

Observe, observe, observe

Keenly observe everything that is happening around you. This will tell you a lot about your company and where it is headed or the external cultural differences that you will need to adapt to. Observe how people dress, how people talk, what is important to people, how work gets done, what your leaders are saying and how your company is being driven. It is essential that you suspend judgement of right or wrong, good or bad. You must only observe and learn.

Be willing to experiment

Times of change and transition present us with the opportunity to do things differently. There is much that you will learn if you have an open mind. Be willing to try new ways of doing things. Be open to meeting and getting to know new and different people. Try to learn a new language and explore new cuisines offered in a new region. Be willing to change how you dress. Adaptation doesn't make you insincere or a fraud. Experimentation will help you get to where you need to get faster and help with career success.

Build on who you are and what you know

Adaptation doesn't mean that you change everything about you. Remember, you were given this job or role because someone thought that you were good enough for it, and that you had the knowledge, skills and abilities to do the work. Some amount of self-doubt is inevitable whenever we are learning new things. But don't give in to self-doubt. Focus on doing your job to the best of your abilities.

As you experiment, observe yourself in action. Take the time to introspect and reflect on what comes easily to you versus what seems more difficult. Seek feedback from trusted colleagues and friends on how you are doing. Most importantly, take time to relax and de-stress.

Throughout your corporate career, you will face many changes and transitions. How you respond to these changes and handle yourself through the transition will determine how successful your career will be. So, embrace your new reality and don't seek to escape the change.

Career progression happens through a series of choices that we make about whether to stay on and continue with a current job or organization, or to do something else. These decisions are sometimes professional and sometimes personal. Sometimes leaving is the right choice, and sometimes staying put is.

Tips and Takeaways

- Career transitions are periods of stress and anxiety. Fight or flight reactions are quite common during this time.
- Transition is the inner psychological process of adapting to the external changes. Remember, every transition begins with an ending – learning to let go of the familiar and embracing a new reality is your path to success.
- You can accelerate the process of transition by becoming aware of your reactions and making a conscious effort to adapt to new attitudes and behaviours.

four

Look Beyond

The world around is changing. These changes will be far-reaching and will impact both the way business is done and the way careers will develop. Preparing yourself is key.

10

WHEN TO STAY, WHEN TO GO

Building careers is hard work indeed, and along the way you will need to make many choices. These choices will be an expression of who you are. The dilemmas you will face will range from whether you want to leave a job that treats you poorly or whether you want to (at least for some time) prioritize your personal life over your career (such as moving to be near family, for health-related reasons, to be in a less intense work environment, and so on).

As your life goes through its inevitable share of times that are tough or times that are a breeze, you will need to develop your own anchors for making these choices based on what you value most in life. As you have perhaps heard us repeat a few times – the most joyful lives are designed and not just achieved. They match your life choices to your deepest joys.

A popular course at Stanford University led by Prof. Bill Burnett and Prof. Dave Evans looks at how one can design a 'well-lived, joyful' life. While we have not participated in their course, we have read their book *Designing Your Life*[1] (and recommend it) and would like to share a few key ideas from their book with you.

1. Instead of expecting success to make you happy (it doesn't), design a life around the things that you love.
2. Your overall sense of well-being in life will come from work, love, health and play. You can design a dashboard for yourself that allows you to assess where you are on each of these and where you would like to be.
3. To build a life that works well for you, articulate your life view (your ideas around what makes life worthwhile) and your work view (what work means to you). These form your internal compass to navigate your life choices.
4. Search for what allows you to 'be in moments of flow' (when you are totally engaged and sense that time almost stops). These moments of flow have a very special place in designing a life of joy.
5. As you try your hand at many activities, pause and reflect on which of these truly energize you and which drain you. The activities that energize you are the ones you want to build on.
6. At the start of your career, you are still trying to learn more about yourself in different situations. Try out many different things. Learn from them and move on.

In the previous chapter, we spoke about the many shifts that lie ahead for each one of you. In this chapter, we share our own unique experiences and the factors that influenced our choices, so that you can begin to think of your own personal guiding principles.

Shalini's story

As you navigate the many crossroads you will encounter in your career, it is helpful to know what you really care about. I have been at a crossroads time and again in my life, and each time I find myself overwhelmed by it. During these moments, I find it very hard to make decisions. It is especially difficult weighing the pros and cons of a scenario where there is an imbalance of information. You may have adequate information regarding one choice, but very limited information about another.

When my mind has been going back and forth between two attractive choices, I have found it helpful to take a moment, quieten the mind as much as possible, before making a decision. After that, I try and see which possibility connects with some of my deepest values. Looking back, I find I have made choices based on four different criteria at various points in my life.

Personal considerations

Early in my career, I made many choices based on personal considerations. Because both my husband and I were working, this meant that sometimes I was the trailing spouse. When I had a very young family, it was important for me to be there for them. I would search for work that gave me flexible hours while allowing me to work in the field of organization development. This meant I pretty much had to create my own opportunities. As a result, I did a lot of interesting work where I learnt a lot, and those were the right choices at the time for me.

Learning opportunities

Once my kids were old enough to begin preschool, I started making choices with a very strong focus on how much I could learn while in the role. I wanted to become an expert in my field and I was searching for opportunities that would teach me something important. I was also somewhat conscious of how a role would look on my résumé. By this time I felt I needed to make choices that would make it easier for employers to hire me.

Yet, my own pull towards learning was often far stronger than careerist choices. And so, I went to University of California, Los Angeles, to do a mid-career PhD in organizational behaviour. These choices sometimes made it harder for employers to understand me as my background was so unconventional, but it allowed me the space to find my own voice.

Self-expression

My choice of work now is often linked to opportunities for self-expression. I find I am very good at working with complex organizational challenges, particularly ones that need a very deep understanding of human behaviour. I find such projects deeply satisfying, and fortunately, my clients also seem to value my contributions. Besides working with organizations, I also love working one-on-one with individuals. I find great personal joy in working with people either through formal coaching, mentoring engagements or even in more informal conversations.

Being able to contribute to the ideas in my field through writing or speaking engagements also allows me to find room for self-expression. At this stage of my career, my desire for self-expression is very strong, and therefore, it guides all that I plan to do as an entrepreneur.

Commercial criteria

Making a good salary has always been very important to me. After all, raising a family requires resources. Kids need to go to college and a household needs money to run. Plus, I have always been a bit scared of running out of money when I retire. Despite the importance I have traditionally placed on money, I have usually been miserable when money has been the primary reason for taking on a job. I have felt fearful and a bit suffocated, as if my wings had been clipped. As a result, I have realized a job works best for me if money is a secondary criteria.

However, now as an entrepreneur, money is also an indication of how my work is valued. When I feel an organization values my work, I am really at my best and do my most creative work. I know that I have expertise in my field and I am very proud of it. Therefore, I focus on projects that are high-value and have space for strong creative expression.

Pradnya's story

During the course of my life, I've changed many jobs, and moved cities, companies and countries. On one level, I was always grateful for the vast number of choices that I had available. On another level, these choices brought with them the dilemmas of having to decide what the 'right' thing to do was and further, having to live with the 'what if' of paths not taken. Making choices when I was younger seemed clearer and easier. As I grew older, as family concerns became more important, choices required much deeper reflection on what I really wanted and what I was willing to let go of. I came to two critical, career-defining crossroads in the first five years of my career.

Getting married and moving cities

I was living and working in Dallas, Texas, when I first met my husband. I was working for Lucent Technologies, earning well and enjoying my job. My fiancé was working a full-time job in New York City and pursuing his PhD at Columbia at the time. Very soon we found that we had to make the decision regarding who would move to the other's city. My husband was ready to move to Dallas and complete his doctoral studies long-distance. However, based on my own experience of the challenges of completing a doctorate, I felt he should continue to stay close to campus. I had seen many doctoral students move away and then struggle to complete their degree in time, and so I proposed to move to New York with the hope of finding a job there.

Moving back to India

I had moved to the United States in the late 1980s at the age of 21 to pursue my doctoral studies. Back then, a common path that most Indians took in order to emigrate to the US was to enrol for an advanced university degree. When I met my husband, he had been living and working in the US far longer than I had, and was on his way to becoming a naturalized US citizen. I, on the other hand, had always wanted to return to India.

Through my family network, I landed a great job in India that also paid well. My husband, however, had work commitments in the US and wasn't going to be able to move immediately. And there we were, back at a crossroads: was I to give up my job, and thus a real opportunity to move back to India, or would we have to live in different countries until he could move back?

I decided to accept the job and my husband followed a year later, after he had wrapped up work in the US and had figured out what he could do in India. This allowed us to keep a route back to the US open while I adjusted to being in India. Once I was somewhat settled in India, it became easier for my husband to let go of our life in the US and relocate. I have encountered several crossroads later on in my career as well. Some decisions were strictly professional, and some were once again very personal.

When the shoe begins to pinch

Sometimes, jobs become like a shoe that pinches you. You know that you are going to get painful blisters unless you take the shoe off. This has happened to me on at least two occasions. In one situation, the job kept evolving due to organizational changes, and after a few years I realized that neither was I interested in doing the job nor did I have the skills and competencies to what the job now required. It was in both my and the organization's best interest for me to graciously move on. Moving on opened up a whole new set of opportunities that wouldn't have come my way if had I tried to stay on, suffering the pain of being in an ill-fitting role.

In another situation, I got caught in a fallout between my boss and the CEO of the company. I enjoyed a great working relationship with my manager, who was the HR Head of the company I worked in. When a new CEO came in and my boss and he couldn't see eye-to-eye on matters, she left the company. The political headwinds were beyond my ability to manage or navigate and it made more sense for me to leave. I moved to a role that gave me the opportunity to build something new, where I felt valued. As a result, I continued to learn and grow.

Other crossroads that some of you may encounter is regarding the decision to live abroad or not.

Living abroad versus returning home

I had already made the decision to return to India once. But after about eight years of living in India, our careers took my husband and me back to the US. This time, the move involved our school-going children. The children were resilient and they adapted quickly to their new environment. However, within a few years I began to feel homesick and wanted to return to India. I missed my parents and as they were getting no younger I wanted to be closer to them. So once again, we moved back. Fortunately, my husband and I have been able to make these cross-country moves relatively easily. This is not the case for everyone, and these decisions are not easy.

Some of you will be faced with the choice of working in another country. See it as a great learning opportunity. If you have deep roots in India there will always be a pull back to the country. If you decide to never leave or choose to return to

India, know that you can build a very fulfilling and rewarding life right here.

Am I a generalist or a specialist?

The field of human resources has what is known as a generalist career path or a specialist career path. My field of study is industrial-organizational (I-O) psychology. Many of you may know of it as business psychology. It's a specialized area, but upon returning to India, I let go of my professional specialization and embraced general HR roles. I took up jobs as an HR leader and grew to love the field of human resource management. But my identity remained anchored in I-O psychology. In 2005, Microsoft offered me the opportunity to build a specialist talent, leadership and organization development function within HR, and I jumped to take it. Instead of continuing to build a career as a general HR executive, I changed gears and got back to being a specialist within the field of HR. Today I own and run a business that is quite anchored in the scientist-practitioner principles of I-O psychology.

Off the record

When you are just starting out, you may not really know what your strengths are. Treat all experiences at work as experiments designed to teach you more about yourself.

As you grow in your career, you will be faced with similar choices. Do I want to be a generalist or a specialist in my function? Do I want to remain a functional expert or pursue a general management career path? Imagine yourself saying at a party sometime in the future, 'I used to be an engineer, but now I'm a people manager/general manager and I thoroughly enjoy it!' As your professional identities shift and evolve, so will your career preferences. Become aware of these changes and follow your inner voice. Living in consonance with your identity is always far more fulfilling. It's never too early to start building a point of view around what will help you make the 'right' decision.

Navigating career crossroads: A careerist perspective

You're now acquainted with our personal journeys, and know that our decisions were based on both personal and professional considerations. These decisions reflected what we cared most deeply about, including a love for learning, wanting to be an expert and our commitment to our families. When making a decision, it is always helpful to have certain parameters in mind and ensure that these yardsticks evolve with you as a person. That way, one is able to ensure that all decisions are made in a collected manner, with all considerations taken into account. You will find that while certain priorities will never change, others will be modified according to where you are in life.

Only you can know the right way to design your career, but in this section we add a few practical tips you might find useful for navigating your own career crossroads.

Evolve guiding principles

Begin to evolve a set of guiding principles for your career. These guiding principles should be anchored in whatever it is that you care deeply about. For instance, do you want a high-profile career? Do you want to keep learning? Do you want to make a lot of money? Do you want to balance career with family? Do you want to have fun at work? Now, while our instinctive response might be to want each of these things, the reality is that each of these criteria will most likely pull in a different direction. Your choices will therefore depend on which criterion you care more deeply about.

For instance, if you want a high-profile career, it means making choices that will place you in the running for these roles. You may need to strategically map out high-impact roles to get you to these positions and focus on getting visibility within these roles. It will mean often putting work ahead of your family and that your work-life balance will be tilted to accommodate more work. It may also mean moving to wherever the best opportunities are for you. On the other hand, if you want a career where you build a reputation as an expert, then you have to pursue whatever opportunities will bring you that expertise and credentials. You will need to seek roles that allow you to develop strong subject matter expertise. For someone else, the best choice may be one in which they are able to balance their family and their work life. They may feel most fulfilled when they have enough time to be with loved ones.

As we discussed right at the beginning of this chapter, what is right for you will depend on what you care about most in work and in life (your life view and work view), how you want your life's dashboard to read (work, love, health and play) and what kind of work brings you into a state of flow where you find maximum satisfaction. But from a purely careerist point of view, is there a right time to move from a role?

Right time to move

It is possible to get comfortable and stay too long in a particular role, and we have seen this happen time and again. As people stay on too long in a role, their choices begin to look a lot like stagnation or lack of ambition. Employers want to see evidence of a growing and evolving career to believe that you have the potential for senior roles.

If you have been in the same role for over five years, it is time to consider whether you are really growing. Now, if you work for an organization that has seen tremendous growth, the answer may well be yes. In that case, your role would have dramatically changed in complexity and scale. However, if the organization itself hasn't seen great growth, you may have stopped growing in your role and it may be a good time to move.

It takes most people about 18 months to become effective in a role, and most of the learning from that experience happens in the first three years. So, after three years in any one role, you may want to consider what you want to do next. Of course, as you move into more senior roles, this period may grow longer as you take time to shape the organizations you lead. Many top leadership roles in large organizations do require time before one can truly make an impact. Be reflective and make good choices based on your context.

Another decision that you will make is whether to stay in one organization or build your career across several organizations. There is no right answer to that. There are many people who have built successful careers following both paths. Take a good look at where your organization is in terms of growth and evaluate if there is scope for you to grow along with it as well as what your growth with them already has been like before you decide to stay for the long haul.

Moving to another organization

You can choose whether to build your career in one organization or across several organizations. It is becoming less common for people to spend their whole working lives within one organization, but it is still possible. The success rate of homegrown CEOs (individuals who have risen the ranks within the company) is considerably higher than CEOs hired from outside. This is an important factor to consider when you are making the decision to stay longer within one organization.

As you stay on with an organization, you will understand its culture better and be influenced by it. You have the opportunity to develop many allies who can keep you informed of any important developments and back you up in all that you do. Of course, you may have networks with critical suppliers or customers that make you very impactful and effective.

If you are working for an organization that you like, and it is a successful one, it is a great idea to spend some time growing your career here. Several successful CEOs have done exactly this. By the time they head the organization, they have experienced several roles within it and therefore have deep knowledge and expertise of how to make the organization succeed. They have reputation and followership in the organization right from the start and can make very impactful leaders.

> **Off the record**
>
> Often you really understand what a job brings out in you only once you get there. Don't agonize. Do the best you can, and if things don't work out...move on.

However, you may have many good reasons to build your career across several organizations too, and this is also a good idea. For instance, you may find your growth blocked in your organization for any number of reasons. This could be because the organization is a small one and does not need people with deeper experience. It could also be an organization that is going through a downturn and is laying people off. You could also have a bad relationship with your own leadership team. Or you could find that your next role requires you to move cities and you may not be able to make the change at that point. It may also be that you just want to experience different organizations and different industries to build a broad base of experiences, and that is fine too.

Most people working today will probably build their careers across several organizations. Wherever possible, keep in mind that you will be telling a story about your career and why you made the choices you did at some stage. It is very important that you are not seen as someone who needed to keep moving jobs because they were unsuccessful in each role. Recruiters are wary of hiring people who have found it difficult to succeed in the past. Career profiles that combine stability and growth are the most attractive to recruiters. If you are able to demonstrate success in a wide variety of organizations, it makes you a very attractive candidate to recruiters.

What do I do if I want to move but simply can't?

Your career will evolve as you make choices about whether to stay or leave a role or an organization. Sometimes, you may find yourself in the wrong role. At times, the organizational culture may not be a good fit for you. At others, the political dynamics of the organization might be such that you are unable to manage or navigate through them. Sometimes, for personal reasons, you may be seeking something different. If you recognize this, it's probably time for you to move on.

However, leaving is not always a choice that you can make, and sometimes you need to stay on even when you don't want to. Market conditions may not be conducive for a move, or family obligations may not give you the freedom to make that choice. These situations are usually extremely frustrating and can generate a lot of anxiety about your performance.

If the only choice is to stay put, then the first step is to become fully aware of the situation and acknowledge it for what it is. It's absolutely okay to stay put in a job because leaving is not a choice that you can or wish to exercise at the time. Almost everyone finds themselves in such a position at some point.

The next step is to manage your emotions and do whatever it takes to bring a positive spirit to work every day. Commit to improving what you can and learn to live with what you cannot. If things really do not seem to be improving, you must start thinking about other options in preparation for a possible worsening of the situation.

In conclusion, always accept that your career will go through many transitions. In this chapter, we gave you two ways to think about your career. We spoke about what it takes to design a joyful career and life – one that is deeply integrated with your life view and designed around those activities that bring you joy. Recognizing what you value in life (more broadly) and in work (more specifically) is important here. The idea is to design a life that builds from the activities that bring you energy and flow. And we do believe that doing so will be extremely rewarding for you in the long run. In the end, the most satisfying careers are often designed and

not just achieved. They are designed around that which will bring you the most fulfilment.

Tips and Takeaways

- When going through every new experience, think of how energized you felt through the experience. By becoming observant of what makes you feel the most energized, you develop keen insights into what will work best for you.
- What matters most is how well your choices match what you really value in life. Big mismatches will leave you unhappy even if you are successful.
- Pay attention to your life as a whole when you are at a crossroads. It is completely okay to make different choices at different times in your life.
- Only you really can know what brings you joy. At the end of the day, only you are in charge of designing the life you want.

11

A BRAVE NEW WORLD

There is no question about it. We know that the future will look nothing like the present.

No other generation in human history will experience technology-led change as far-reaching as the present generation will. As a result, this generation will have to be prepared to reinvent themselves as drastically. A study by the Institute for the Future (IFTF)[1] suggests that as many as 85 per cent of the jobs that will exist in 2030 haven't been invented as yet. There are few markers to give us any idea on how organizations and their structures will evolve.

You must have heard talk about how artificial intelligence (AI) will impact the way jobs are designed, how the education system will need to undergo a major overhaul in order to be able to cater to the job market of the future and how changing social structures could influence employment opportunities. For a young professional this may feel a bit overwhelming. And if so, that's

completely normal. Our world is changing faster than it is perhaps possible to keep pace with. However, one thing is for sure – it will not be possible to stay insulated from any of these changes for too long. Those starting their careers now will have to find a way to ride the waves of these changes time and again.

Have we been here before?

This is not the first time that technology has fundamentally altered the way human societies live and work. In fact, according to the World Economic Forum, there have been three industrial revolutions so far. Each revolution has had very profound consequences not just for the way we work but also for how human societies have lived.

Almost without exception, those who study future trends predict that the fourth industrial revolution will transform our work and lives in ways that are going to be even more game-changing than the previous revolutions. We are just beginning to understand the details of how these changes will play out, and you can be sure that this generation will witness some of the most dramatic changes of our times. What is different about this revolution is just how much is expected to change in a very short period of time. You can read the book *The Fourth Industrial Revolution* by Gideon Rose for insights on how economists and policy makers at the World Economic Forum in 2016 approached this phenomenon.

So, what are the technological changes driving this revolution? One of the key factors is that several new technologies are maturing around the same time, including artificial intelligence, robotics, 3D printing, the internet of things, nanotechnology and driverless cars. Technologies that were, until very recently, within the realm of science fiction are fast becoming a reality. The consequences of the arrival of these new technologies are very dramatic, and they have huge implications for the way industries and organizations operate. Think of how online streaming of content has fundamentally altered the shape of the entertainment business or how Uber has fundamentally changed the shape of local transport. Think of how many more disruptions lie ahead with the arrival of driverless cars or hyperloop commutes.

The highly connected nature of our globalized world means that these changes will take place far quicker than before. Electricity arrived in India in the early 1900s and the Taj Mahal Palace hotel in erstwhile Bombay was the first hotel to use electricity.[2] And yet, it has taken over a hundred years for electricity to reach all the villages in India. Contrast this with the use of mobile phones. In just a few decades, mobile phones have reached even the most remote parts of the country. Or, look at the adoption of the smartphone. Introduced over a decade ago, it took just five to seven years for the widespread adoption of these devices. The rapid pace at which new technologies are adopted is important because it suggests that we might see revolutionary shifts fairly quickly.

What's next?

So what do we know about what lies ahead? Unfortunately, no one has a crystal ball that can tell us for certain what will happen next, but these are some trends that careful observers agree on.

Large-scale automation

The automation of existing work will perhaps be the most obvious change you can expect to see. There will be an impact on blue-collar jobs because of advanced robotics, and for the first time, white-collar jobs will also come under pressure on a large scale. Pretty much any work that relies on systematic thinking and decision-making is a potential candidate for automation. Business research reports in a number of leading publications suggest that, at least to start with, we are likely to see more and more human decision-making supported by technology rather than by people. That means that part of the work done by people right now will be substituted by technology.

Most studies suggest that this automation will have profound implications as the number of humans needed to produce a particular product or service will become fewer. There has been much discussion around which kind of work is likely to be most impacted. Currently, conventional wisdom holds that work that requires high levels of emotional intelligence or creativity will be relatively hard to automate. However, given the high levels of emotional intelligence displayed by some of the most advanced AI, we will need to wait and watch.

Large-scale automation has many implications for the kinds of skills that you will need to develop through your career. As more and more work is powered by technology, you will need to make conscious choices about the strengths that you bring to a job. A study on the future of work by McKinsey & Company in 2017[3] suggests that in around 60 per cent of occupations as much as 30 per cent of the activities will be automated.

Large-scale disruption

Another outcome of new technologies maturing is that they provide new ways to solve old problems, and these new ways disrupt the way industries are organized. Think about how Uber and Ola have disrupted the taxi industry. Prior to their arrival, your options as a customer were limited to the closest taxi stand. You could not choose what kind of vehicle you wanted to ride in, nor was pricing at a competitive level. For the most part, traveling by taxi was fairly expensive. But a host of new technologies (and a brand-new business model) allowed Uber and Ola to develop a new way of solving a very old problem. Of course, to get to this point, a number of other technologies had needed to mature – the smartphone, mobile data connectivity, GPS technology, to name a few.

The reason this example is so interesting is because it shows how a host of new technologies can solve an existing need in a new format. The taxi industry does not qualify as a high-tech industry, and yet no one could have foreseen how a widespread adoption of technology could have changed its face forever. As new technologies mature, we can expect widespread disruption of entire industries, and it won't be limited to high-technology fields. So, one thing seems very likely – you will experience first-hand disruption at close quarters.

> **Off the record**
>
> Perhaps the best way to view the future is to think of the unlimited opportunities it holds. But remember, you will have to create opportunities for yourself.

Human–technology combine

While the mechanization of work began over a hundred years ago with the Industrial Revolution, it has taken a very long time for technology to reach the levels of sophistication that compete with human abilities. You may have already watched videos of Sophia, the robot made by Hanson Robotics. Sophia gives us a glimpse of what the future holds in the field of human-like robotics. This is very different from the mechanical arms and legs being used in various factories for the last couple of decades.

What makes this generation of robotics so different from those that came before is their human-like qualities. They are aesthetically appealing, well-mannered and intelligent – unsurprisingly, since Sophia is said to be modelled after Audrey Hepburn. While Sophia has become a cultural phenomenon, what is so fascinating about this development is that it opens the door for more human-like robots. In October 2017, Sophia was the first robot to be awarded citizenship anywhere in the world by Saudi Arabia. The website of Hanson Robotics states,

> Dr Hanson aspired to create genius machines that will surpass human intelligence. Dr Hanson believes that three distinctively human traits must be integrated into the artificial intelligence of these genius machines: creativity, empathy, and compassion. As an extension of human intelligence, Hanson Robotics' genius machines can evolve to solve world problems too complex for humans to solve themselves. Sophia personifies this bold and responsible goal.[4]

More recently, Japan in its Robot Strategy has set a goal to ensure that 80 per cent of elderly care recipients will receive some form of robotic assistance by 2020.[5] Granted that the cost of implementation will be very high, these are likely to be very basic robots, but this can still cause a large amount of disruption in the world of caregiving. We are still likely to see the boundary between humans and technology blur more and more. This implies that a key requirement of most future jobs will be to understand the technologies of that field and figure out how they can best be leveraged for the organization.

New organizational forms

The modern organizational form that we are most familiar with emerged from the need to manage scale and alignment of operations across multiple product lines and multiple geographies. But we are already seeing a new organizational form emerge with the operations of companies like Airbnb or Uber: the network organization, a unique organizational form that relies on a large network of entrepreneurial partners who aren't directly employed by the company.

At the heart of this form of organization is a robust technology platform that integrates operations across time zones and locations. Such organization is agile, scalable and replicable. Judging by the success of Airbnb and Uber, we are likely to see this organizational form being used by many more people than ever before. What this means is that there might be fewer people working with salaries, pay scales, promotions and learning and development support. There will, however, be far more people working for an organization as entrepreneurs. This form of organization has many implications for the kinds of careers in the future, as it opens up self-employment to many. Since the initial principal amount required is far lower than what traditional entrepreneurial jobs require, this business model is a lucrative one.

What does this mean for you?

At the outset, let us say that we are too early in the fourth industrial revolution for anyone to really know the exact shape of things to come. In fact, predictions being made at this point may play out quite differently in the future. A famous example recalls Thomas Watson, the former chairman of IBM, once being asked about the number of computers that would be demanded in 1943. He said, 'I think there is a world market for maybe five computers.' Of course, we all know how accurate that prediction was!

> **Off the record**
>
> Organizations are becoming leaner and smaller at their core. There are fewer employees in the setup. Most other people associated with it will be part of the organization's network – not its core.

However, there seem to be some broad principles emerging for how careers will play out in a time of great change.

It will be very hard to remain mediocre, but it will be a great time to be exceptional.

Over the past couple of decades, technology has allowed entrepreneurs to accomplish success as would have been unimaginable just a few decades before. We are likely to see that success will only accelerate. Entrepreneurs who can think of new ways of addressing customer needs will find many opportunities for great growth. The growth of social media, for example, has enabled people to become stars overnight if they possess something that others want to see or hear.

It will be a great time to be unique and exceptional. However, if you are average, then things may become harder as you compete with technology for work that is less distinctive. The easiest tasks to be automated are those that follow a reasonably predictable format. At a recent workshop on creativity, Shalini asked a team of about 80 engineers whether they largely used the right side of their brains or the left. Many of them started laughing and said that they do not use their brain at all. Now, while this was a joke, hidden behind this is the reality that many of today's jobs do not expect, or even encourage, the independent use of one's thinking faculties. As more companies develop an augmented workforce, and with technology looking after the work that is predictable, you will need to keep a few steps ahead by bringing in your unique thinking. Technology has the potential to augment your competence. And exceptional abilities will allow all those who work at their field to build great careers.

Your ability to keep learning will matter considerably

For the past decade or so, learning agility, or the ability to learn from every new experience and then put that learning into practice, has been what differentiates those who will lead from the others. In other words, if you have high levels of learning agility, you will be able to draw insights from every experience you go through (positive or negative), and use that learning to change what you do next.[6]

This will be doubly true for those entering the workforce now. As industries face continuous disruption and as jobs get transformed, the future belongs to those who can keep learning and adapting. While organizations themselves may take the lead in educating and re-skilling their workforce, the future belongs to those who are actively involved in shaping their own learning. This is because any organization will only teach you that which is useful for it, but you will need to learn that which will be useful for you. So, think about your strategy to remain a lifelong learner and think outside the usual degree programmes – these are not the only ways to learn. In fact, being high on learning agility has more to do with your ability to extract learning from your experiences at work and translate those into new ways of doing things.

> **Off the record**
>
> For the right person, this is going to be a very liberating time. Keep learning, keep growing and keep evolving.

Take the case of two people working in the exact same role, say that of an area sales manager. The person with high learning agility will keep reflecting on their experiences each day and learning from them. They will figure out better ways to work with customers, craft pitches, maybe even distribute products in their territory. Their low-agility counterpart will continue to put in the hard work and yet, do pretty much the same thing each day. It is not hard to figure out who will achieve greater success in their career.

Resilience will be more important than ever

Continuous change can be exciting, but it can also be stressful. Combine that with the fact that you will probably experience many career shifts through your working years, and we come to what will be the foundation of success over the next 30 years: resilience.

Resilience, or the ability to bounce back after difficulties in life, is a quality that can be learnt through an interesting combination of optimism, perspective, faith, self-care and support. Resilience is similar to a muscle – the more you exercise resilience, the more you are able to be resilient.

So how can you build your personal resilience? The answer lies in building your own personal support systems (like family and friends), setting up good self-care practices (exercise, sleep, nutrition, meditation, etc.) and adopting a philosophy of life that allows you to keep learning from experiences and see setbacks as temporary in the larger tapestry of life.

Today, many organizations recognize the importance of resilience and are teaching their senior leaders how to develop it. For those of you who are starting your career now, resilience will be more important than ever. How you will handle the inevitable challenges of life will be influenced a great deal by how you interpret them. If you are able to interpret setbacks as challenges to bounce back from, you will be able to handle them well. You may also be able to find ways to keep rekindling your hope in the light of changing circumstances. This grounded optimism will be your best friend. Nurture it carefully.

The American Psychological Association has listed several helpful habits to build personal resilience, which you can look up. For this and more resources on building resilience, please check the notes at the end of this book.

Building a career in a brave new world

The brave new world you are entering now holds wonderful promise. You will have opportunities that no previous generation ever had. Your generation will experience one of the greatest fluxes in the history of the world. For some of you this will mean great opportunities, and for most of you it will mean great change.

It is our hope that you now understand that there is a different set of skills that will become critical for those starting out in their careers at this time. These are the skills of being able to keep evolving, keep growing and be resilient in the face of challenges. Many of you will not be able to rely on corporate careers alone. There is already much talk of an evolving gig economy where professionals will come together for projects and then move away from the organization once that work is done. Such work can be quite exciting because it liberates you from the shackles of operating in a rigid organizational structure. Successful gig workers are essentially entrepreneurs and will need all the skills of a successful entrepreneur – great interpersonal skills, great marketing skills and quick learning ability. Much like entrepreneurs, they will essentially need to be self-starters who are constantly searching for the next big opportunity and finding ways to bring their talents to this opportunity.

All signs therefore point to a world where your careers will be far more self-directed than careers of the past. It will also be likely that you will experience many organizational changes and disruptions. That is where learning agility and resilience will become the cornerstones to your wonderful career.

Tips and Takeaways

- As you build your career, become the key driver of your own learning and growth. Few organizations will do this for you.
- You may need to be far more self-reliant in designing your career than any generation in the past. Traditional organizational ladders are fast vanishing.
- There will be far more uncertainty and far more opportunity than ever before. This is very exciting and may also be unsettling.
- By being at the forefront of thinking of ways in which technology can help your business, you may become very valuable to the organization.

12

TWENTY QUESTIONS ON CAREERS

The biggest issue that faces many of us once we enter the workforce is figuring out if we fit in. A career tends to be long and it is rarely going to be linear. Most of us battle with career dilemmas and constantly question whether we are in the right jobs. Our priorities are varied – salary, passion and convenience – and our expectations are manifold. For the most part, you will have to find your own answers, but here are a couple of questions that were fielded to us that we think will help ease the process of transition.

As you will see, there is no one answer. Often, asking the right questions is the only benchmark you will have to assure yourself that you are heading in the right direction.

1. What should I do if I don't feel valued at work?

Shalini: You may feel like you are not being valued at work at different points in your career. Sometimes, it is simply because you are working for a boss who isn't very expressive of their appreciation. If that is the case, you may just have to accept that aspect of their personality.

If, on the other hand, you receive many signals that you are not welcome in an organization over a long period of time, you should take notice. Some of these signs are: not being called in for important meetings, not being involved in critical decisions or not being marked on emails that concern you. If this is the case, you are genuinely being sidelined. Think about what you would like to do about this. If you are working for an organization that you really love or if you are not in a position to move at this time, you may have to wait it out. But don't wait this out longer than necessary. Speak to others in the organization who think well of you. See if you can move to another team or seek involvement in another project where you have the opportunity to showcase your talents.

Pradnya: We feel most valued when our work is appreciated. When you first join a job, people are often watching you to see what you are capable of, how much initiative you are taking and hence, how much work they can really give you. During this initial period, you may feel that you are not being challenged enough or that your inputs are not being taken seriously. Once you have shown that you can deliver results and that you are interested in taking on more work, work will come to you. If you still feel undervalued or not taken seriously, ask your manager for a meeting and discuss your feelings. Perhaps you will get some feedback on what else you should be doing. It may be the case that the organization needs you to gain more experience before giving you a higher level of work, so build a roadmap of how to get there. If none of this works, then perhaps you don't really fit in with either the role or the organization, and may be better off somewhere else.

2. How do I create appropriate visibility for what I am doing?

Shalini: This is a very important part of being recognized within an organization. In very large global organizations, it is easy for your work to get lost if you don't have a boss who wants to create visibility for you. If your work fits into a larger initiative in the organization, it is a good idea to seek out leaders responsible for that initiative and make them aware of the work you are doing. Wherever it makes sense, you can ask team leaders if you can make presentations for them or for their teams to showcase the work you are doing.

Other ways to create visibility are to keep senior leaders in the loop regarding any big project you are working on. You can seek their advice and share your progress regularly. Keep in mind that this is effective only if the work you are doing is genuinely good. Otherwise, you will be creating visibility for poor work, and that will not work well for you.

Pradnya: Before creating visibility, make sure that you are seen as reliable by doing your work properly and on time. Whatever work is given to you, do it well. Show that you are ready to take on more challenging work, and ask for it. Keep your manager informed about what you are doing. Short, precise emails, quick phone calls, brief one-on-one chats are easy ways to keep your manager informed. You should not assume that he/she knows what you are working on. If your company has a practice of skip-level meetings (meetings with your manager's manager), ask for such interactions. When senior leaders from other locations are visiting your office and there are town hall meetings or other interaction opportunities, make time to participate. Go prepared to ask a question, should the opportunity arise. When opportunities arise for volunteer work or to get involved in cross-functional, cross-team work, raise your hand. These are opportunities that help build visibility for you and your work beyond your immediate team.

Your personality will often play a role in how easily these behaviours come to you. Extroverted people with higher sociability generally find it easier to connect or create visibility for themselves. Ensure that you are not coming on too strong or as a show-off. On the other hand, if you tend to hold back in social interactions, you may need to change your natural style. Building visibility is a slow, systematic process. Don't be in a hurry or feel like you need to grab centre stage right away. At the same time, don't unduly hold back either.

3. How do I ask for what I need at work?

Shalini: There is a fine balance between asking for too much and asking for too little. If you keep asking for resources that others in situations like yours don't really need, you come across as someone who lacks resourcefulness or is making excuses. However, if you don't ask for resources you genuinely need, your project will fail and that can be worse. Learn how to make a good case for the resources you need and present a well-thought-out plan that has considered ways to manage with fewer resources.

Pradnya: Be straightforward about what you need. Demonstrate what you are good at and how you have been contributing to work. Make a case for why you deserve to get what you need. Remain open to others' points of view and attempt to meet people in the middle.

4. What do I do if I make a mistake at work?

Shalini: From time to time, you are likely to make mistakes, and in most organizations, that is all right. Good organizations do understand that you are just learning the ropes in the early years. As long as there is evidence that you are able to learn from your mistake and keep improving, you should be fine.

Occasionally, you may slip up and make a mistake that has many repercussions. In such a case, it is best to alert your team and bosses at the very earliest so that your mistake does not snowball and lead to greater problems down the road. In such cases, it helps if you can demonstrate that you regret the incident and are going to do all that you can to set things right. In fact when a mistake is handled very well, it can build greater faith in your abilities.

Pradnya: When you are new to a job, mistakes are bound to happen. The best strategy to adopt when you make a mistake is to accept responsibility. If at all possible, reflect on what you could've done differently and be prepared with ideas to mitigate the damage. I've made many mistakes in life. Some mistakes have cost me dearly, while others have only been minor setbacks. Some bosses will be more tolerant of mistakes and others less so. Accept whatever yelling, scolding, blaming you are getting and take it in your stride.

Mistakes present tremendous opportunities for learning and growth. But if you find yourself making too many mistakes, step back and reflect. Do you have the skills to do the job or do you need more training? Is it that you don't find the work interesting and hence are unable to focus? Do you understand what is expected from you or are the directions from your manager unclear? Or is it something else?

5. How do I keep learning when my job takes all my time?

Shalini: Now that is a difficult question to answer, and it is one that you will have to find your own answer to. No one can afford to just keep doing their role without stepping back and continuously developing their skills any more. It is likely that the capacity to continuously learn will, in fact, become even more critical in times to come.

Different people learn differently. For some people, learning comes from reading books and reflecting on what they have read. For others, it comes from talking to more experienced and knowledgeable people. And for some it comes only by experiencing something new or different on the job. If that is you, keep thinking of what you can do differently in your role to deepen your expertise.

Just as you create your KRAs for the year, create your personal learning goals as well. Use technology to help you find the right resources online. These could be courses, YouTube videos, books or Google alerts. Learn whatever you like, but remember to keep growing.

Pradnya: This is a very common challenge. Most of your learning will come on the job from doing your work, being mentored by senior colleagues or learning from your manager. There will be times when you will want to supplement your learning by taking appropriate courses. Don't always expect your employer to pay for these courses. Have an annual learning budget, and invest in yourself. You will see that the investment will pay off. This has worked for me and for many others who I work with. You may need to use your vacation time or weekends to attend some of these courses. If the learning is related to your work and the employer does not need to pay for it, managers will be amenable to allowing you to take time off.

Sometimes, what you learn may be directly related to your work. At other times, it may be a hobby, a skill, or an area of knowledge that you've been wanting to dive deep into for a while. What you learn is far less important than having an annual learning goal and to follow through on it with the same discipline as you would a business or performance goal. As we discussed earlier in the book, the speed of obsolescence for technology and people is increasing. Only a lifelong learning habit will help with sustained success.

6. Should I do only what I've been asked to, or do more?

Shalini: It is always a plus if you are able to exceed expectations and do more than what is required of you. Realistically, your ability to do this may vary depending on how much of a stretch the original targets were. Wherever possible, go above and beyond a task. Not only will you be developing skills, you will also build a reputation as a solid performer.

Pradnya: Definitely do what you have been asked to do and do it well. You should certainly show initiative and ask for more challenging work, but only after you have demonstrated success in your assigned work and built some level of mastery.

7. How do I deal with an insecure boss?

Shalini: Insecure bosses need to know that you will not do anything to upstage them. Consult them frequently so that they feel like they are always on top of things. Sometimes, the best way to deal with an insecure boss is to recognize the cause of their insecurity and then go out of your way to help them feel safe around you. You could do this by frequently sharing information that they would not otherwise have access to or by giving them a lot of credit for guiding the work that you are doing.

Pradnya: There could be many reasons for your manager feeling insecure, and it will probably have nothing to do with you personally. As you will see, building a solid working partnership with your manager is important for both your success. You will find many useful tips in the chapter 'Managing the Boss' to help you with this.

8. What if I believe that the top management team is incompetent?

Shalini: I would say this is a red flag. If your organization is not doing well and the general word on the street is that your organization does not have a strong future, you may want to look elsewhere for opportunities.

Pradnya: Before you jump to the conclusion that the entire top management of the company you are working for is incompetent, talk to a few people in the industry. That will help you get perspective on the business challenges that the senior team is trying to deal with. You may not agree with the way that they are handling things, but they may have their reasons for doing it. However, if you lose faith in the competence of the entire senior management of the company you work for, it is time to look for a new job.

9. How much should I really care about what happens in other teams?

Shalini: It helps to have a sense of the goings-on in other teams so that you have an idea of how the work that you do connects with the organization at large. You do not need to know every detail on a daily basis, but having a sense of what they do is very helpful. It will help you come up with good projects and ideas, and also help you develop a broader perspective of the business, which is very helpful as you become more senior.

Pradnya: A lot of the work in organizations today crosses team boundaries, and it is rare for your team to be an isolated island. So, it is always a good idea to build relations with people in other teams. This may also help you get on cross-functional teams and do interesting work that expands your skills and creates broader visibility for you.

10. Do my educational qualifications matter?

Shalini: This varies from one organization to the other. In general though, it matters far less within your organization than it does in an external search mandate. People in your organization know you, and while they may be aware of your educational qualifications, they also have a great sense of what you are capable of. Search mandates, however, often include specific educational qualifications. If you do not meet these educational qualifications, recruiting firms may not reach out to you.

Pradnya: Education opens doors in your chosen career. It gives you foundational knowledge and an entry into the field. Some fields require ongoing learning like medicine, chartered accountancy and law, among others. When people wish to change their careers, course work and education becomes critical. As discussed earlier, even for general managerial jobs, cultivating a habit of lifelong learning is valuable.

11. Is it possible to climb the corporate ladder without stepping on other people's toes?

Shalini: Yes, it is absolutely possible to be nice and climb the corporate ladder. In fact, if you are generally well liked, it will help you be effective. What you have to be conscious of is that you keep doing very well in strong roles, building a good track record for yourself. You must develop the ability to spot projects or roles that give you space to perform, and then give it your all. In addition to building a great track record, it always helps to be aware of the general politics of the environment you are in as it will help you avoid awkward situations.

Pradnya: Absolutely! Remain focused on building your strengths and moving forward. Growth does not mean that you have to trample on others or bring them down to get ahead.

12. When do recruiters doubt my commitment to a job? How often is too often to move?

Shalini: There are no hard and fast rules here. Instead, there is a range. For instance, most recruiters in India tend to see three years as an acceptable tenure in a role. However, through the course of your career you will very likely have some longer stints in certain organizations and a few shorter ones. When you are in a good organization where there is scope for growth, seek opportunities within the company first. You will be more effective because you know the organization, and you can build credibility and depth.

Pradnya: Recruiters look for logical, coherent movements. As an HR leader, I am generally okay with résumés that show quicker job changes early in their career and then have slowed down. Early-career job changes help build different skills and competencies. If you are a mid-career professional, it is important to also show that you have contributed to the growth of the organization. At senior levels, showing that you have stayed steady through different business cycles builds credibility.

A rule of thumb that I like to use is that generally, you are learning in the first year in an organization; the second year is when you begin to contribute; and the third year is when you can deepen your competence, or begin to think of movement to your next role. Remember that early in your career, the job scope may be limited and you may reach peak performance within 12 months, in which case, moving to another role within 24 months may be logical.

13. If I take a break from corporate life, will I get rehired?

Shalini: Well it depends on how long you were away and what skills you gained while you were gone. But for the most part, the answer today is yes. It may sometimes take longer to find a job, and sometimes you may have to start with an organization or role that is not your first choice. In fact, if you have had a very good career profile in general, taking a break and then doing something productive in that time may even add to your distinctive story.

Pradnya: If the break was for a reason that you can share with others, people are quite willing to rehire you. A break usually helps you either build a new skillset or take care of personal requirements (personal illness, illness in the family, aging parents, childbearing). You may feel that others who started their careers with you and didn't take a break have raced ahead, and that is probably true. But as long as you are committed to your work and your growth as a professional, you will eventually catch up.

14. Do women have to work harder to succeed?

Shalini: This is a very sensitive subject, but I think that is very often the case. Part of the reason why they struggle is because of the additional work that women do when they become mothers. But that is not all. Women often have to work harder to establish credibility. There is a very strong body of research that shows that both men and women undervalue women's work and that people are more critical of women's leadership style. So that does make it harder. Having said that, there is nothing that can stop a woman who has found her own voice and purpose.

Pradnya: Unfortunately, the workplace in general is not a level playing field. As we discussed earlier, gender-related biases are prevalent across organizations. Women are also often playing the lead role in running the home and raising kids. As a result, at times, it does feel like women have to work harder to succeed.

15. Can both husband and wife have a grand career?

Shalini: Yes, absolutely. Both of you would need to support each other and be especially understanding of each other's needs. There are many well-known examples of both spouses having built extraordinary careers. You just have to make sure you are always there to support each other. It often helps to build additional support systems for when both of you need to be away at work.

Pradnya: Yes, they can. It requires a strong partnership and an equal commitment to the other person's career as you have to your own career. If children are involved, it also requires equal partnership while parenting. The biggest challenges for dual-career couples arise when relocation decisions are to be made. Different couples solve the problem differently. My husband and I have lived in different countries, sometimes for years, in order to support each other's professional aspirations, and I'm seeing more and more dual-career couples doing this nowadays. It does put a strain on the relationship; my children have wondered if their parents were splitting up. These issues need to be handled with care and sensitivity. At the end of the day, it is about balancing a commitment to yourself and a commitment to your spouse and the family unit.

16. Are children a liability when building successful careers?

Shalini: Not at all. Balancing raising a family with a successful career is certainly a challenge, particularly for dual-career families. But many people manage it well. Particular moments, like when a child is sick or going through a rough patch, can be very hard, but you can certainly find ways to work around these challenges.

Pradnya: I've never found children to be a liability. My two children have brought me tremendous joy. I have also learnt very important life skills from parenting – patience, tolerance, unconditional love, nurturing, discipline and surrendering my ego. For women, the challenge is sometimes greater as they have to go through nine months of pregnancy, nursing and then get back to work. But with more family-friendly policies, things are getting somewhat better. Do try to build a support system to help you with raising your children – doing it all alone can be quite difficult and strenuous.

17. How much fun is it to be at the top of the organization?

Shalini: This varies a great deal from person to person. There are some who relish the responsibility and power that comes from the top job. For others, it feels like a burden. So it depends on who you are and what your deepest needs are. Being a chief HR officer is certainly very different from any other HR role because for everything related to HR the buck firmly stops with you. There is definitely a sense of heightened responsibility. On the one hand, there is great joy in having the authority to make important changes while on the other hand, you want to be sure that you are making the best choices. For me, it helped to have a set of senior HR advisers outside the company to use as a sounding board from time to time.

Pradnya: If you enjoy taking responsibility for others and for outcomes, the top job is a lot of fun. If you don't, it can become stressful. Life at the top is not a cake walk, and it requires a lot of hard work, commitment and personal sacrifices. You have a lot of privilege but there is also a lot of responsibility.

18. What if the company I wish to work for doesn't come for campus recruitment?

Shalini: Then you'll need to make the extra effort to reach out. Some organizations have very limited entry points or only hire from a few specific colleges. If you cannot enter through these points it is certainly going to influence the odds of you getting a job in that company. But there are multiple entry routes into an organization. Just get a sense of where you will fit in vis-à-vis other fresh recruits and make sure that you are comfortable with that.

Pradnya: If it is a company that you are really interested in, try to network with people who are working there and make inroads. Sometimes, it is a good idea to go through the campus interview process to find your first job, even if it is in another company. After you have spent an appropriate amount of time there and gained some experience (two to three years), you will move into the category of an experienced, lateral hire. Don't give up on your dream. Doors may open at a different level later on in the company of your choice. Use this time to build a network of relationships in the company you wish to work for.

19. Can I trust Glassdoor ratings?

Shalini: Only up to a point. There have been recent reports that some companies persuade employees who are likely to post positive reviews to write about their experience in order to bolster ratings from time to time.[1] So be careful of Glassdoor data and track it over time. Don't trust it completely as it could be influenced by reviews over a short period of time.

Pradnya: Anything in the public domain that is not edited or fact-checked is always open to manipulation or even falsification. Treat Glassdoor ratings as one source of data. They will give you some insight into a company's culture, but it's best to find your own primary sources of information about the company. If you are considering joining a company, talk to people who are working there. Ask questions during your interview and then judge for yourself.

20. How careful should I be on social media?

Shalini: If there is something you absolutely do not want anyone at work to be aware of, don't post it on social media at all. It is hard to completely erase anything you have posted on the internet, so exercise discretion there. Organizations vary a great deal in the extent to which they track your social media profiles. However, that doesn't mean that you can't post regular life events.

On the other hand, if you have no social media profile, not even a LinkedIn profile, many recruiters will be a bit wary. Having a LinkedIn account is generally a positive thing even if you are not very active on it. I recently met a recruiter for a prestigious international programme who shared that one way they vetted candidates was by checking their LinkedIn profiles and that they were not comfortable proceeding with candidates who had no contacts.

Pradnya: Social media is an advertisement of brand You. In the same way that you would not be casual about your company's brand on the internet, be conscious about your social media presence, because what you post on LinkedIn, Instagram, Twitter or your preferred social media platform is likely to be seen by others and judged by them.

13

LAST WORDS

There is so much more to life than work. Your health, your relationships, your other interests are all important to living a fulfilling life.

Yet for many of us, our fulfilment at work (or the lack of it) spills over to our experience of life in general. We spend so many of our waking hours either at work, getting to work or thinking about it, that our overall sense of well-being is impacted.

We like the Japanese idea of *ikigai* to help design our careers around work that is deeply satisfying.

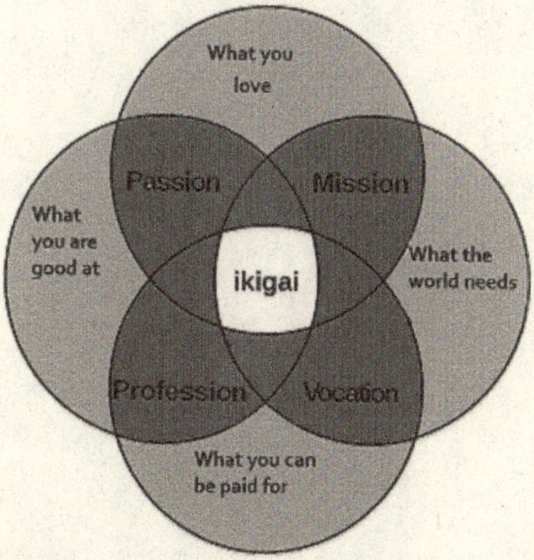

(By Nimbosa. Derived from works by Dennis Bodor and Emmy van Deurzen. Source: Wikimedia Commons[1])

The framework is simple – it is a philosophy to help you find your motivation both for your work and on a daily basis. Your *ikigai* is the point of intersection of what you love, what you are good at, what the world needs and what you can be paid for. Our own personal sweet spot or *ikigai* is not always immediately obvious.

Think of this as a lifelong quest – perhaps one of the most important quests of all. And in case you are wondering if this sweet spot exists – it does. And it's a beautiful place to be in.

It has taken us a few decades to get closer to our own personal sweet spots, but it is our hope that you will be way smarter. After all, you are starting your careers off with a 'secret' understanding of your organization that we simply didn't know of.

Here's to your joyful and fulfilling career!

NOTES

Chapter 1: Iceberg Tips and Unseen Blips

1. Edgar H. Schein, *Organizational Culture and Leadership: A Dynamic View*. Massachussetts: Sloan School of Management, MIT, 1988.
2. Arthur L. Stinchcombe, 'Social Structure and Organizations', in *Handbook of Organizations*, ed. James G. March. Chicago: Rand McNally & Co., 1965, pp. 142–93. The idea of the founders' blueprint was introduced in this seminal article that speaks about how organizations form and the implications of the early decisions.

Chapter 2: Myth in Our Midst

1. Rohit Deshpande and Anjali Raina, 'The Ordinary Heroes of the Taj', *Harvard Business Review* 89, no. 12, 2011.

Chapter 3: Think Business

1. Strategyzer, 'The Business Model Canvas'. Accessed from https://www.strategyzer.com/canvas/business-model-canvas. The business model canvas is an excellent way to understand any business. Strategyzer has wonderful books that describe

in detail the most important questions to ask, and is a great resource for anyone who wants to understand business.

2. Benjamin Graham and Spencer B. Meredith, *The Interpretation of Financial Statements*. New York: Harper Business, 1998.

Chapter 4: Building Ties

1. Douglas Stone, Bruce Patton and Sheila Heen, *Difficult Conversations: How to Discuss What Matters Most*, Penguin Books, 2010.

Chapter 5: Managing the Boss

1. John J. Gabarro and John P. Kotter, 'Managing Your Boss', *Harvard Business Review*, January 2005.

Chapter 6: Power and Politics

1. S.F. Brosnan and F.B.M. de Waal, 'Monkeys Reject Unequal Pay', *Nature* 425 (2003): 297–99.
2. Cade Massey, 'Specialization Achieving Personal and Professional Success', *Influence*, Wharton School of the University of Pennsylvania. Web.
3. Mark S. Granovetter, 'The Strength of Weak Ties', *American Journal of Sociology* 78, no. 6 (1973): 1360–80.
4. M.R. Endsley, 'Toward a Theory of Situation Awareness in Dynamic Systems', Human Factors Journal 37(1), 32--64, March 1995.

Chapter 7: Men and Women

1. International Labour Organization, Global Wage Report 2018.
2. Peggy Hazard, Dési Kimmins and Benjamin Frost, 'The Real Gap: Fixing the Gender Pay Divide', *Korn Ferry Institute*, 10 May 2016.

3. Sheryl Sandberg, *Lean In: Women, Work, and the Will to Lead.* New York: Alfred A. Knopf, 2013.
4. For an insight into how unconscious biases get set up, read Lesley Symons and Herminia Ibbarra, 'What the Scarcity of Women in Business Case Studies Really Looks Like', *Harvard Business Review,* April 2014.
5. Curt Rice, 'How Blind Auditions Help Orchestras to Eliminate Gender Bias', *Guardian,* October 2013.
6. Read more about Professor Frank Flynn's experience with the Heidi and Howard Roizen case here: Joanne Martin, 'Gender-Related Material in the New Core Curriculum', speech at WIM Banquet, 2007.
7. Z. Estes, 'Confidence Mediates the Sex Difference in Mental Rotation Performance', *Sydney Felker Arch Sex Behav* 41 (2012): 557–70.
8. K. Kay and C. Shipman, *The Confidence Code: The Science and Art of Self-Assurance—What Women Should Know.* New York: Harper Business, 2014. This is an excellent read, particularly for women who want to develop their self-confidence.
9. Adrienne B. Hancock and Benjamin A. Rubin, 'Influence of Communication Partner's Gender on Language', *Journal of Language and Social Psychology* 34, no. 1 (2014): 46–64.
10. T. Jacobi and D. Schweers, 'Justice, Interrupted: The Effect of Gender, Ideology and Seniority at Supreme Court Oral Arguments' 103 Virginia Law Review 1379 (2017). Northwestern Law & Econ research paper no. 17-03.
11. American Supreme Court Justice Ruth Bader Ginsburg on how to work through interruptions: Kimberly Weisul, 'How Ruth Bader Ginsburg Cut Down on the Supreme Court's "Manterrupting"', *Inc.*, 2017.

Chapter 8: Know Thyself

1. The Big Five personality traits model was defined by several independent sets of researchers. The initial model was advanced by Raymond Cattel with 16 fundamental factors of personality being proposed. Robert McCrae and Paul Costa later developed the Five-Factor Model, or FFM, which describes personality in terms of five broad factors.
2. Robert Hogan and Joyce Hogan, 'Motive, Values Preferences Inventory: The Inside of Personality', *Hogan*, 2013.
3. Robert Hogan and Joyce Hogan, 'Reflections on the Dark Side', *Hogan*, 2015.
4. Marshall Goldsmith, *What Got You Here Won't Get You There: How Successful People Become Even More Successful*. London: Profile Books, 2013.
5. Tomas Chamorro-Premuzic, *The Talent Delusion: Why Data, Not Intuition, Is the Key to Unlocking Human Potential*. London: Hachette, 2017.

Chapter 9: Embrace Change

1. William Bridges with Susan Bridges, *Managing Transitions: Making the Most of Change*. London: Nicholas Brealey Publishing, 1995.

Chapter 10: When to Stay, When to Go

1. Bill Burnett and Dave Evans, *Designing Your Life: How to Build a Well-Lived, Joyful Life*. New York: Random House, 2016.

Chapter 11: A Brave New World

1. Institute for the Future (IFTF), 'The Next Era of Human/Machine Partnerships: Emerging Technologies' Impact on Society & Work in 2030', trans. Dell Technologies, 2017.

2. 'Tata Titans: Jamsetji Tata', *Tata*, Web. Accessed from http://www.tata.com/aboutus/articlesinside/An-icon-and-an-ideal
3. James Manyika, 'What Is the Future of Work?', McKinsey Global Institute, December 2017. Accessed from https://www.mckinsey.com/global-themes/future-of-organizations-and-work/what-is-the-future-of-work
4. 'Sophia: A.I.', *Robinson Speakers*, 30 April 2018. Sophia of Hanson Robotics has been attracting tremendous attention across the world. You can watch her here: http://www.hansonrobotics.com/robot/sophia/
5. Daniel Hurst, 'Japan Lays Groundwork for Boom in Robot Carers', *Guardian*, 6 February 2018.
6. Both the Center for Creative Leadership and Korn Ferry Associates have a number of white papers on learning agility available online. You can read some here:
   Ron Rabin, 'Blended Learning for Leadership: The CCL Approach', Centre for Creative Leadership, 2015.
   May Knight and Natalie Wong, 'The Organisational X Factor: Learning Agility', White Paper, Focus, Korn Ferry, 2018.

Chapter 12: Questions on Careers

1. Rolfe Winkler and Andrea Fuller, 'How Companies Secretly Boost Their Glassdoor Ratings', *Wall Street Journal*, 22 January 2019.

Last Words

1. Graphic representation by @emmyzen (Emmy van Deurzen). Source: https://t.co/TiRhcMD7HP. Authored by Nimbosa, derived from works in public domain by Dennis Bodor (SVG) and Emmy van Deurzen (JPG). Source: https://commons.wikimedia.org/wiki/File:Ikigai-EN.svg

Further reading

Listed here are other readings that will be useful for those wishing to read more on the topics discussed within the book.

1. J. Martin, M.S. Feldman, M.J. Hatch and S.B. Sitkin, 'The Uniqueness Paradox in Organizational Stories', Administrative Science Quarterly 28, no. 3 (1983): 438–53.
2. S. Kleinfield, The Biggest Company on Earth: A Profile of AT&T. New York. Holt, Rinehart and Winston, 1981.
3. Andrew Tobias, Fire and Ice. New York: William Morrow, 1976.
4. O. Schisgall, Eyes on Tomorrow. New York: Doubleday, 1981.
5. Ittelson, Thomas R., *Financial Statements: A Step-by-Step Guide to Understanding and Creating Financial Reports.* New Jersey: Career Press, 1998.
6. Mullis, Darrell and Judith Orloff, *The Accounting Game: Basic Accounting Fresh from the Lemonade Stand*, Naperville: Sourcebooks, 2008.
7. The World Economic Forum and most of the global strategy firms have come up with their own sets of predictions around the form this will take. There are many different perspectives and it is too early to say which will play out. But here is a good read about the fourth industrial revolution: Gideon Rose, *The Fourth Industrial Revolution: A Davos Reader*, New York: Council on Foreign Relations, 2016.
8. The speed of adoption of technology has been increasing at an increasing rate. Read more here: Rick Rieder, 'Tech Adoption Rates Have Reached Dizzying Heights', Market Realist, December 2015.
9. American Psychological Association lists several ways to build resilience in your own life. Read 'The Road to Resilience', *American Psychological Association*, Web.

10. There is a popular article by Tara Parker-Pope on building resilience when you are middle aged. Read Tara Parker-Pope, 'How to Build Resilience in Midlife', *New York Times*, 25 July 2017.
11. In a book co-authored with Wharton professor Adam Grant, Sheryl Sandberg discusses life after the loss of her husband and what she has learnt about resilience in the process. Sheryl Sandberg and A.M. Grant, *Option B: Facing Adversity, Building Resilience, and Finding Joy*, New York: Alfred A. Knopf, 2017.
12. Angela Duckworth, *Grit: The Power of Passion and Perseverance*, New York: Scribner/Simon & Schuster, 2016. This book is a great read describing what differentiates those who make it big from those who give up very soon. Angela also has a very popular TEDTalk that you can watch here: https://www.ted.com/talks/angela_lee_duckworth_grit_the_power_of_passion_and_perseverance?language=en

ACKNOWLEDGEMENTS

There are many people who have helped us create this book, in their own different way.

Our first thanks are to each other. We are also thankful to Poulomi Chatterjee for believing in the book and aligning us as first-time authors; Ansila Thomas for being our first critic, adviser and editor; and Niyati Dhuldhoya for being a painstaking editor and forcing us to make changes even when we didn't want to.

There are many others who have contributed their time and ideas to the book. Suvojoy Sengupta for sharing ideas on how to understand organizations, Arvind Raghavan for helping us understand the legal framework of sexual harassment, Krish Shankar, Amit Nandi, Apurv Nagpal, Ravi Gilani, Rakesh Chopra and Rohtash Mal for allowing us to interview them in order to understand how careers are built.

Many thanks to our friends, family and colleagues for all their support and encouragement rendered at various stages of the book.

Shalini and *Pradnya*

***

Pradnya, thank you for joining me on this journey. What would I have done without your deep understanding of what makes people act the way they do. Thank you, Rashmi Bansal, Madhuri Y. and Lira Priyadarshini for your moral support for the book. What would life be without such good friends. You mean so much to me.

My thanks to my husband, Kabeer, for always being there and supporting me in building my own career; my parents for always encouraging me to dream big and study hard. I am in fact, one of many writers in the family. Many thanks to my grandmom, my mom and my father-in-law who are accomplished authors and have been trailblazers for the rest of us; and my in-laws for always understanding my dreams. Thanks to my sister for raising the bar of writing standards so high. You always give me a reason to shoot even higher.

A special thanks to my kids. I want you to know that a life well lived is one that you will create for yourself, in your own signature way. I wish for you the joy of losing yourself in work that you love and find meaningful, time and again. Thank you for your constant questioning of how far along I was with my writing. You kept me going even when I thought I was done.

Shalini

***

Shalini, thank you for inviting me to be a part of this exciting creation. I have enjoyed your creative mind and fresh new ways of thinking.

My thanks to my mother for giving me the passion to read. I grew up watching my mother who was prolific in her reading and writing. Her writing reflects her command of the Marathi language, her knowledge of Sanskrit and her deep understanding of world literature.

To my angel, my daughter Shruti, who is also my voice of conscience. You bring me so much love and joy. To the three men in my life – my father, my son and my husband – you have been my cheerleaders and silent supporters for everything I have done and aspire to do in life. You guys are the wind beneath my wings.

And last, but not the least, my team at Three Fish who made it possible for me to take the time out to write this book.

Pradnya